Contents

KU-613-235

Acknowledgements

The authors would like to thank their families for their support and encouragement.

The authors and publishers wish to thank the following who have kindly given permission for the use of copyright material: the Asthma Society and Friends of the Asthma Research Council for an article from *Asthma News*, 15 July 1987; Hodder & Stoughton Ltd for an extract from *Quest for Adventure* by Chris Bonington; the *Independent* for articles; Mintel Publications Ltd for statistical information; NOP Market Research Limited for an extract from a 1984 survey in Sheffield to investigate women's leisure time; Ian Serraillier for 'The Diver', © 1963; *Sport and Leisure* for an article from the July–August 1985 issue; Times Newspapers Limited for an article by Rob Hughes, 20 November 1986.

The authors and publishers wish to acknowledge the following photograph sources: All-Sport pp. 64 (right), 68 (bottom), 73 (bottom right), cover; BBC Hulton Picture Library pp. 73 (top left, bottom left), 75, 76 (top left), 77; Jim Brownbill pp. 45, 86; Camera Press pp. 58 (left), 68 (left, top, centre), 72 (right), 89, 102, 104; John Evans p. 91; Richard and Sally Greenhill pp. 4, 16, 17, 18, 19, 31, 33, 36, 50, 51, 92, 93, 115; N. Hammond pp. 94, 114; Tommy Hindley p. 67; The Keystone Collection pp. 64 (left), 68 (centre), 69 (centre top, centre bottom), 90, 95, 97, 101 (top, bottom left); Mansell Collection p. 76 (top right); Popperfoto pp. 66, 69 (left, right), 76 (bottom left); *Pretoria News* p. 85; Sporting Pictures (UK) Ltd p. 58 (right); Times Newspapers Ltd p. 99; Topham Picture Library pp. 68 (centre), 72 (left), 76 (bottom right), 80, 101 (bottom right), 103.

The publishers have made every effort to trace the copyright holders, but where they have failed to do so they will be pleased to make the necessary arrangements at the first opportunity.

SPORT ASSIGNMENTS

Paul Beashel and John Taylor

**MACMILLAN
EDUCATION**

First published 1988

Published by
MACMILLAN EDUCATION LTD
Houndmills, Basingstoke, Hampshire RG21 2XS
and London
Companies and representatives
throughout the world

Designed by Raynor Design
Long Compton
Warwickshire

Typeset by Wessex Typesetters
(Division of The Eastern Press Ltd)
Frome, Somerset

Printed in Great Britain by
Richard Clay Ltd, Bungay, Suffolk

British Library Cataloguing in Publication Data
Beashel, Paul
Sport assignments.
1. Sports & games. Social aspects
I. Title   II. Taylor, John, *1942*–
306'.48
ISBN 0–333–45422–7

Introduction

If you want to learn to swim the only way is to get into the water and try. You will not learn merely by reading about it, listening to lectures on it or watching it on television.

We believe that the same active approach should be used when learning about sport. Although you will find some information in this book, you will also find numerous questions for you to answer, problems for you to solve and assignments for you to complete.

You will seek out information from a wide variety of sources, discuss your findings with others and develop some original ideas of your own. You will be involved in all of the following approaches to learning if you undertake the complete set of modules:

Survey of individual interests and needs

Survey of community needs

Local investigations and extended studies

Case studies of local provision for leisure and recreation

Visits to local leisure and recreation centres

Surveys of local businesses associated with leisure and recreation

Work experience and work shadowing

Visiting speakers from local clubs and organisations

Promotion of events and participation in them within the school, college or local community

Primary research involving interviewing and questioning a wide variety of practitioners in the field of leisure and recreation

Secondary research through the use of libraries and other secondary sources of information

Studies of local media and information services

Design and production of publicity material and visual displays

All the above will involve you in communicating with others in a wide variety of situations:

questioning, discussing, explaining, disagreeing and clarifying. You will also have to produce written reports, write letters and articles and calculate the financial costs of many of your decisions. You will work by yourself as well as in group situations involving role play and simulations.

If you tackle all of the tasks positively then you will be sure to learn a great deal about sport. You should also develop a number of other skills essential for success in working life. The world of sport is very wide. This book contains a selection of areas relating particularly to the management, administration and vocational aspects of sport. A companion volume will deal with physical fitness, training and assessment, the psychological aspects of sport and skill acquisition.

Each module stands on its own, but all the modules contain a number of interwoven strands which enable you to use the ideas and information gained in one module in order to enhance the quality of work you achieve in each of the others. The three appendices give detailed guidance on how to obtain information, how to display it, and a list of useful addresses. The grid on the next page indicates the sporting areas which each module covers.

Whether you are following a GCSE Physical Education course, a CPVE sport and leisure option or one of the many other sport and leisure courses, then you should find a large number of the modules very relevant to your needs.

The following grid indicates which of the more general skills are likely to be developed in each of the various modules. The grid should only be used as a guideline however. The degree to which students develop their skills of communication or problem-solving will depend on how they tackle any particular module or assignment. The grid will be particularly useful when a student is evaluating what he or she has achieved in a particular assignment. It should also help in the formation of profiling statements.

Areas of sport covered by individual modules

	Self assessment	Fitness and training	First aid and injuries	Health hazards	Benefits of sport	Administration of sport	Economics of sport	Working in sport	Current issues	History of sport	Sporting officials	Politics of sport
1 Planning – getting it right					✓	✓	✓	✓	✓			✓
2 Running a sports club				✓	✓	✓	✓	✓	✓		✓	
3 Working in a sports centre	✓		✓	✓	✓	✓	✓	✓	✓		✓	✓
4 The Grapefruit Health and Fitness Club	✓	✓	✓		✓	✓	✓	✓				
5 Sport for all			✓	✓	✓		✓		✓			
6 Blowing the whistle						✓	✓	✓	✓			✓
7 The economics of sport						✓	✓	✓	✓			
8 Sports equipment							✓					
9 The magic sponge			✓	✓		✓	✓	✓				
10 Sporting origins						✓			✓	✓		✓
11 Britain's sporting past						✓	✓		✓	✓		✓
12 Sport as a political football						✓	✓		✓	✓		✓
13 The Minister for Women								✓	✓			✓
14 Sport reported						✓						
15 What price excellence?	✓	✓	✓	✓	✓							
16 Outdoor pursuits	✓	✓	✓	✓	✓			✓				

CPVE core area checklist

	Personal and career development	Industrial, social and environmental studies	Communication	Numeracy	Science and technology	Information technology	Creative development	Practical skills	Problem solving
1 Planning – getting it right		✓	✓	✓	✓			✓	✓
2 Running a sports club		✓	✓	✓				✓	✓
3 Working in a sports centre	✓	✓	✓	✓				✓	✓
4 The Grapefruit Health and Fitness Club	✓	✓	✓		✓			✓	✓
5 Sport for all		✓	✓	✓	✓				✓
6 Blowing the whistle			✓	✓			✓	✓	✓
7 The economics of sport	✓	✓	✓	✓				✓	✓
8 Sports equipment	✓	✓	✓	✓		✓	✓	✓	✓
9 The magic sponge		✓	✓	✓					✓
10 Sporting origins			✓				✓	✓	✓
11 Britain's sporting past		✓	✓				✓	✓	✓
12 Sport as a political football		✓	✓		✓			✓	✓
13 The Minister for Women	✓	✓	✓	✓				✓	✓
14 Sport reported		✓	✓				✓	✓	✓
15 What price excellence?	✓		✓					✓	✓
16 Outdoor pursuits			✓					✓	✓

Planning – getting it right

AIMS

To gain knowledge and understanding of:

- sporting facilities and their usage in the local community
- the sporting activities and hopes of the local community
- how an adequate provision of sporting facilities could benefit the local community

To develop the skills of:

- obtaining information from a variety of sources, including questionnaires and interviews
- map compilation and graphical representation
- presenting an effective report using a variety of methods

Imagine that your town had won the prize money. You need to prepare a plan for spending the money.

Local Sports Council Scoops the Jackpot

Glenwood's sports centre manager Colin Blake, received the shock of his life when he heard on Friday that the centre had taken first prize in the Sports Council's 'Centre Management' national competition. This means that the local Sports Council will receive a grant of one million pounds to improve the town of Glenwood's sports facilities. The only condition is that the plans are acceptable to the Sports Council.

 Assignment 1

Use maps of your town and the surrounding area to produce a radial chart, showing the direction and distances of sporting facilities from the centre of town.

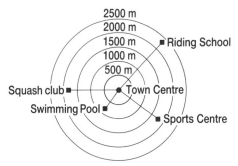

Use a separate map to shade in housing areas, playing fields, parks and recreation grounds.

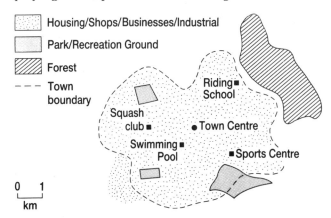

Assignment 2

List the major sports facilities in your town and
comment on the ease of access using a chart like the
one below.

FACILITY	Travel by car including parking facilities	Travel by public transport	Proximity to town centre	Access scale 1–5 easy–difficult
Swimming pool	On the main road. A large car park	Regular bus service. 5 mins walk from station	15 mins walk	1
Squash club	Minor roads, long queues early evening. No car park; difficult to find parking early evening	10 mins walk from nearest bus stop. 30 mins walk from station	45 mins walk	4

 Assignment 3

Compile a summary of the sports facilities in the
town and comment on the standard of each facility
and possible improvements as in the chart below.
Take photographs or make sketches of the facilities
if possible.

FACILITY	Number	Comments	Possible development
Tennis courts	20	6 in good condition at private club. 14 in 2 recreation grounds in poor repair	Improve facilities at one site. Convert other courts to hard areas for five-a-side football, roller hockey etc. in association with nearby youth club

Sometimes there can be a big difference between the standard of local, amateur facilities and national, professional facilities.

Assignment 4

Conduct a survey at one of your town's major sports facilities to find out how:

 (i) people travel to the facility
 (ii) far people travel to the facility
 (iii) often people travel to the facility
 (iv) people would like the facilities improved

It will only be possible to sample the users of the facility. Care must be taken not to choose untypical times and days. Your summary might be similar to this:

```
FACILITY              Glenwood Sports Centre

DATE AND TIME         7.30 - 8.30 pm
OF SURVEY             Thursday evening

ACTIVITIES            Five-a-side football,
TAKING PLACE          weight training,
AT THE TIME           aerobics
```

No. of people interviewed............37

Mode of travel

```
Walking.................................10
Car.....................................18
Public transport........................8
Other...................................1
```

Distance travelled

```
Up to 2k................................5
2 - 4k.................................12
4 - 6k..................................8
6 - 8k..................................7
8k+.....................................5
```

Average individual weekly use of facility

```
Once a week............................28
Twice a week............................5
3 times or more.........................4
```

Improvements that people would like to see

```
Add sauna...............................2
Improve weights room....................5
Add tennis courts.......................3
Improve showers........................10
Improve changing room..................17
```

Now present your results in a visual form. (See appendix 2 for details on how to do this.) For example, you might display the distances travelled as a radial chart:

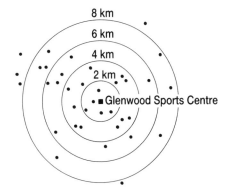

Or you might display the most requested improvements as a pie chart:

Glenwood Sports Centre: most requested improvements

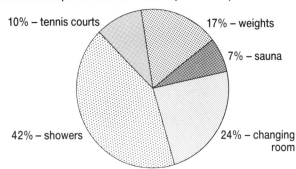

or a bar graph:

Glenwood Sports Centre: most requested improvements

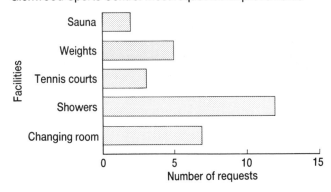

Having gathered together and displayed your information, you should now draw some conclusions. You might consider the following points:

What conclusions can you draw about travelling to the facility?
What new facilities would be most popular?
Do you think these results should be compared with those from a survey of people not at present involved in sport?

Assignment 5

Your survey is likely to show a whole range of desirable improvements to existing facilities and completely new facilities. Find out the cost of improving or building new facilities by contacting the Sports Council, your local authority's recreation department or the many specialist firms in this field. Work out what is included in the cost and what will be an extra. For each facility, consider the potential for generating income to pay running costs.

Here is an example of what one company, Stoners Buildings Ltd, built for the Sun Alliance Insurance Group:

A sports hall complex including a main hall measuring 32m by 17m providing facilities for four badminton courts, tennis court, volleyball, basketball, netball, indoor hockey, five-a-side football and cricket plus a physical conditioning room, together with an equipment store, viewing gallery and entrance lobby. The building was designed and built by Stoners Buildings Ltd in just 24 weeks on the site in 1984 at a cost of £201,000.

They also completed a two-storey clubhouse for Reed International in 1985 in just 15 weeks at a cost of £226,700. This consisted of a clubroom and function room with communicating bar, kitchen, office and toilets on the ground floor, and a billiard room with five changing rooms on the first floor.

 Assignment 6

Potential users of any facility may be estimated by considering the age of the local population. For example, would it be better to site the facility near a new housing estate with many young couples with children or close to a development of expensive retirement bungalows?

Obtain your town's census records from the local library and show the distribution in various forms, including bar chart, pictogram and pie chart (see appendix 2). How will the population distribution in your town affect the siting of new sporting facilities?

 Assignment 7

Submission to Sports Council

Produce a booklet to convince the Sports Council that your plans to spend the £1 million are based on facts and sound judgement.

You should include the following:

  (i) Summary of the current leisure provision.
 (ii) Your proposed list of new facilities in priority order, with site, cost and estimate of future use. Include supporting information on local population, use of sports facilities, willingness to travel and what improvements people would like to see.
(iii) Photographs, drawings, maps and information in tables and graphical form to support your proposal.

You may like to consider making use of videos and tape recordings to put your case more strongly.

SQUELCH!

Assignment 8

The day after you complete your submission to the Sports Council the following letter arrives from France:

From your limited French you know that the writer is trying to develop sporting links between Glenwood and Angers through exchange visits. You may need to get the letter more accurately translated. When this is done, form a small committee from the sports centre to discuss how to reply. Include on your committee Helen Staines, one of your assistant managers who you know is a member of the Glenwood–Angers Association. Write a letter in English to Corinne Faure and draft out proposals to put to the sports centre's management committee for developing sporting links with your twin town.

CLUB L'OLYMPIQUE

Parc de Loisirs du Lac de Maine
Route de Pruniers
49000 Angers
Tel: 41.64.78.02

Mr Colin Blake   Angers, le 15 Avril 1988
Glenwood Sports Centre
Millhall Lane
Glenwood
England

Cher Monsieur Blake,

Je vous écris de la part des amateurs et amatrices de sport du Club l'Olympique d'Angers. Comme vous le savez nos deux villes sont jumelées, et nous aimerions beaucoup établir des liens sportifs entre Glenwood et Angers.

Ici à Angers nous avons un grand centre sportif avec une piscine et de vastes terrains de jeu. À ce centre on peut participer à toutes les activités sportives principales et nous nous intéressons particulièrement au tennis, au hockey au handball et au basketball.

Je sais bien que cela fera grand plaisir à nos membres d'accueillir vos équipes à Angers et aussi d'avoir l'occasion de voyager à Glenwood et de faire votre connaissance.

Dans l'attente d'une réponse favorable, je vous prie d'agréer, Monsieur, mes sentiments les plus distingués.

Corinne Faure

Corinne Faure
Directrice

Running a sports club

AIMS

To increase knowledge and understanding of:

- the structure of a sports club

- the problems associated with running a sports club

- how sports clubs can be successfully managed

To develop the skills of:

- comprehension

- questioning and instructing

- committee work

- decision-making

- problem-solving

- evaluation

Club's Dive To Disaster

For many months the people of Daltringham have wondered what has happened to their sports club, once the pride of the town. Founded just ten years ago it quickly established a reputation in junior rugby with players winning county caps and one an England trial. A soon as a Sunday football section was formed, the club won the local league three times in the first five seasons.

However times have changed dramatically. Last Saturday only one rugby side took the field and, composed largely of veterans and youngsters, it crashed 66–7 as expected. Only two seasons ago five sides were fielded regularly. The two Sunday football teams withdrew from their leagues at Christmas as they were unable to raise full sides each week.

Off the field, the club has been plagued by apathy and financial mismanagement. Although the club still has a long lease on its council pitches, the severe financial problems have cast doubt on its future beyond this season.

Our reporter, Tracy Binns, has been talking to a number of officials who have left the club recently and has established the following facts:

1. The club's dire financial situation first came to light last month when Rex Whaker, the Treasurer, left the club, his wife and family to join his secretary, Amanda Prior, in the Canary Islands.

2. The players lost faith in the Selection Committee after a number of controversial decisions in October last year. This resulted in an exodus of players to Redhouse Park just before Christmas.

3. The pitches and the clubhouse have gone to wrack and ruin since old Fred Lane, a founder member of the club, unofficial groundsman, bar steward and handyman, died suddenly in January.

4. The general management of the club this season has been appalling. Dates of meetings and agenda have not been publicised in advance and it is claimed that important decisions have been made without the necessary majority. Social events have been virtually non-existent, the annual dinner-dance was cancelled and the bar is often closed even on match days. The number of players attending training has fallen dramatically. The disciplinary record is unacceptable. Plans to build squash courts and to develop activities to attract women members and families have been shelved indefinitely.

The people of this town must decide whether or not they want a sports club. Time is running out fast. A special meeting has been called for next week to decide the club's future.

 **Assignment 1**

                                        The Clubhouse,
                                        Daltringham Sports Club,
                                        Ringland Road,
                                        Daltringham

25 March 1987

Mr Trevor Woodhouse,
27 The Glebe,
Daltringham

Dear Mr Woodhouse,

        Thank you very much for the detailed notes you sent me giving
guidelines for the management of clubs such as ours. I am writing to you
now in the hope that you might be able to rescue the club from its desperate
plight. We understand that you have had many years experience with the
Sports Council and that your book 'Club Guidelines' is highly recommended.
Currently there are only three officials left in the office - myself
(Vice-Chairman), Mr Brian Mount, the acting Secretary and Mr Dean Smart,
the manager of the Colts rugby side. We intend calling an Extraordinary
General Meeting next week and would like you to consider nomination as
Chairman. I do hope you will be willing to help us. It would be tragic
for the town if the club went under.

                        Yours sincerely,

                        Thomas J. Sweetingham,
                        Vice-Chairman DSC.

Imagine you are Mr Woodhouse and have just received the above letter, having earlier read the report in the *Daltringham Echo*.

Draft your reply, agreeing to nomination as Chairman. Set out any conditions you wish to be known and request any further information you would like regarding the running of the club.

Assignment 2

Write out a short speech to be delivered to the meeting once you have been elected Chairman. Use the following plan as a guide:

Immediate action

Finance	– investigate situation thoroughly
	– audit books
	– determine current situation
Fixtures	– find out the number remaining to be completed
	– discuss availability of players
Clubhouse	– urgent repairs
	– make sure services (gas, electricity, water) are functioning
Pitches	– make sure they are in playable condition
	– check what equipment is available

Proposals for improvements for next season

Meetings	– regular meetings of executive to plan policy
Committees	– formation to start work
Publicity	– to attract members
Fund raising	– to put club on sound basis
Clubhouse/ ground	– regular working parties
Social events	– to raise both morale and cash

CLUB GUIDELINES
by Trevor Woodhouse

Reasons for members joining

To participate in sport
To mix socially
To improve skill levels
To enjoy competition
To keep fit
To be involved in a club

Club rules

They must be concise, easily understood and not open to misinterpretation.
They should include:

Name and location of club
Aims of the club
Methods of electing members, officers and committees
Financial arrangements
Procedure for annual general meetings

 Assignment 3

Daltringham Sports Club

Founded 1977

Rules

1. That the club be called Daltringham Sports Club and membership shall be open to all.

2. That the club colours be green and yellow.

3. That the officers of the club consist of
   (a) Chairman
   (b) Vice-Chairman

This is the only surviving written record of the rules of the club. Using the extract from the *Club Guidelines*, draw up a set of rules which would cover the current needs of the club members and which could be changed in the future to meet new circumstances.

Meetings

Meetings need:
advance notice, appropriate time and venue
the chairman and secretary present
to follow an agenda
opportunities to speak
to follow voting procedure
to announce decisions

Committees

These will vary with the size, objectives and facilities of the club. They will often include:
management, clubhouse, ground, bar, social, finance, development selection, fund-raising and catering.

Officers

The main officers are Chairman, Secretary, Treasurer. Others may include Auditors, Social Secretary, Membership Secretary, Captains.

Finance

Income	Expenditure
Subscriptions	Rent, rates
Bar profits	Employment of staff
Catering surplus	Maintenance and repairs
Match fees	Fuel and essential services
Hire of club facilities	Insurance
Social events	Hiring equipment and facilities
Revenue from game machines	Costs of aministration
Grants, donations, sponsorship	Fees
Investment interest	Cleaning and laundry
Goods sold	Interest payable

Fund Raising

Social events may include jumble sales, parties, fêtes, dances, race nights, car rally, barbecues, sponsored events, auctions, raffles.

More long-term methods include collection of paper, '100' club, sale of bricks, sale of special memberships, loans and donations.

Developing Facilities

Forward Planning must take into account:

Sports to be catered for
Types of facility required
Links between facilities
Funds available for building and maintenance
Income generated

Building and outdoor facility plans must take into account:

Money available
Activities planned for building/area
Use of building/area
Spectator and specialist facilities
Floor or playing surface requirements
Standard of play anticipated
Maintenance necessary
Additional equipment required

 ## Assignment 4

All clubs of this type are run by committees. The rules of a club will usually say how committees are to be elected. The number and type of committees set up will depend on the size and type of club and any particular needs. Refer back to the *Club Guidelines* on committees and decide the number and type of committees which the club needs, taking into account facilities available at present. For each committee outline its purpose, composition, meetings to be arranged and list of priorities.

List any committees which might be needed to be formed during the next season.

 ## Assignment 5

Fund raising

The financial affairs of the club are in a disastrous state. Urgent action is required. Carry out the following three actions to avert short-term and long-term financial ruin.

1   Assume that enough money can be found from reserves to pay off all outstanding debts but £1,000 is needed to complete this season's fixtures, to make some urgent repairs and to enable the basic services to continue. Draw up a list of activities which might be used to raise this money quickly. For each activity set a target, consider the expenses involved, number of helpers required and the publicity wanted. Produce your plan of action to be considered as soon as possible by the new Chairman.

2   With four other people, set up a fund-raising committee to make plans for the future. You will have to consider what might be attempted during next season and what sort of long-term projects might be established. Draw up your proposals in detail for consideration by the management committee at its next meeting. You will need to fix dates for many activities, consider targets, investigate each enterprise in detail and consider the effort involved related to the profit to be made.

3 Assume that a disco of some sort will be arranged for a Saturday evening at the clubhouse. Working in small groups produce a checklist of items which the organiser could use to ensure that everything is planned in advance and will run smoothly on the night. Possible headings to use would be publicity, music, bar, catering, tickets, safety, parking, local residents, staff.

 Assignment 6

Behaviour of members

Under the chairmanship of Mr Woodhouse, Daltringham Sports Club is halfway through its recovery season, having re-established its membership and improved morale throughout the club.

Following the Christmas holiday period a number of cases have been reported to the Disciplinary Committee for action:

1 Ashley Brown was spoken to a number of times by the referee during a hard game with local rivals Barton RFC. Following remarks made in the dressing room, in the hearing of the referee, he has been formally reported to the county authorities who will take action in due course.

2 On Christmas Eve, five of the third XV attended a disco in town and were ejected following a disagreement between one of the players and an off-duty policeman. The report in the paper mentioned the club by name, although the players were not officially representing the club.

3 J. Halliwell has been a tower of strength for the club in the past, mainly in the first XV. Having been dropped to the second XV he has requested that he be picked in the third XV as, to quote him, 'I'm not playing with that wingeing fairy of a captain just out of nappies.' It is club policy to pick teams on strength.

4 The bar till has been short on three occasions this year. Unfortunately the one person who has been on duty on each of these occasions is Terry Lineham. It is known that unofficially he allowed his 19-year-old son Chris to help him on each occasion. In the past Terry's trustworthiness would never have been questioned.

Roles for disciplinary meeting

ASHLEY BROWN

You have been a pillar of strength in the first XV since moving to the area from Leeds. You have played a lot of amateur rugby league where you gained a reputation as a tough nut. You believe you have calmed down a lot. In Saturday's game you were badly treated by the opposing forwards and given no protection by the referee. This is what you were complaining about, not realising that the referee was present. Later you had three stitches inserted in a head wound.

WAYNE STRINGER

You have been elected by your friends in the third XV to represent them at the Disciplinary Committee meeting. Aged 19, 6 feet 2 inches, and with blond spiky hair you believe that people in authority pick on you. At the Christmas disco you were only trying to separate the hooker, Mike Westfield, from a man who had been taking liberties with his girlfriend. No one knew that he was a policeman and your knee had hit him in the face accidentally. You agree that all five of you had been drinking since 5.30 that evening.

JOHN HALLIWELL

You have been a member of the Daltringham Sports Club for the last eight years and captained the first XV for two seasons in 1983–5. You do not now have so much time to devote to training because your wife has recently given birth to a bouncing baby boy. You still want to play rugby however and feel that the third XV is the team for you.

The Selection Committee want you to play for the second XV because they believe that you are the second-best hooker in the club. You cannot stand

Mike Ferrett, who is the captain of the seconds. He is a young, very good player but, in your opinion, full of his own importance. One of the other reasons for wanting to play for the thirds is that two of your best mates also play for the team and they say that it is great fun, particularly as they win all their games by large margins.

You have always been a person who says what he thinks and does not suffer fools gladly.

You are a drinking friend of Ian Wells who you know is on the Disciplinary Committee.

TERRY LINEHAM

Since your retirement from the rugby field 10 years ago, you have taken an increasingly active interest in the work of the club's bar committee. Indeed you were the one barman over the last couple of seasons who could be relied upon to open the bar at the appointed hour. While your son Chris has been out of work he has offered to help you in the bar, and you have been grateful for his help. Chris has played a few games for the club, but is not very interested in rugby, preferring fast motor bikes and rock music concerts.

In groups, imagine you are the Disciplinary Committee interviewing the player/s involved. Consider each case in turn and bearing in mind club rules and club policy, together with its reputation and unofficial codes of behaviour, come to your decision on the evidence before you.

 Assignment 7

A windfall!

Daltringham Sports Club's recovery has continued throughout the season. Just before Easter the following letter arrived on the Chairman's doormat.

```
                                          P.O. Box 163
                                          Daltringham


   The Chairman
   Daltringham Sports Club
   Ringland Road
   Daltringham


   Dear Mr Woodhouse,

           Congratulations to you and your committee!  I am both amazed and
   delighted at the recovery the Club has achieved this season.  It has long been
   a wish of mine to contribute to the Club in some tangible way, but I have
   hesitated for obvious reasons.

       Having just retired from business, I should be very happy to contribute
   £500,000 for a major additional facility.  My only condition is that it
   should be used to attract lady members and families.

       If my offer is acceptable, please send me full details of your plans
   with an explanation for the decision made.  I regret that I must remain
   anonymous for the present.

                           Yours sincerely,

                           A friend.
```

The Chairman decides to set up a Project Committee to respond to the unknown benefactor's offer. Imagine your group is this committee. In order to make your decision you will need to know answers to the following questions:

(i) What types of facility could be built for the money offered? (For example, squash courts, swimming pool, tennis courts, floodlit all-weather area, weights/conditioning room, hall for badminton etc.) You will need to find out how much these different facilities cost by contacting firms who supply them. Look up their addresses in the Yellow Pages.

(ii) Could additional funds be obtained to increase the size of the gift? For example, you might contact the Sports Council, Local Authority, National Playing Field Association, local companies and industry. Full opportunity should be taken of this once-in-a-lifetime offer. (Warning – beware of financial overcommitment!)

(iii) What additional facilities would be favoured by:
(a) present club members?
(b) families and lady partners of present club members?
(c) people of the town not involved in the club?
Investigate methods of contacting these groups to estimate future likely use of facilities.

(iv) What additional benefits/demands would such a facility bring? For example:
Benefits – more members, greater income, development away from male-dominated sports club, more community involvement.
Demands – extra maintenance costs, loan repayment, more staff, more committees.

When you have completed your investigation draw up a report and a series of proposals to be put before the club as a whole. You will need to give carefully argued reasons for all your decisions.

 Assignment 8

It is the end of the recovery season. With your new project in mind it is essential to increase the membership of the club. You have been set the task of improving links with the local schools and encouraging school leavers to become involved with the club. Carry out the following three actions:

1 List ways in which you could link the club with a local school. As a first step it would be important to convince the head teacher and staff of the school that the club is worth joining. Pupils could be invited to the club in a variety of different ways.

2 Draw out a pamphlet detailing what the club has to offer and the plans for the future. Detail its success in the past, what has been achieved in the last year and the new project. Explain how the club is run, the teams put out each week, the social activities and above all who to contact and how to become involved.

3 Prepare a script for a video programme to be made by the club to show specifically to young people of school-leaving age. Consider the following information when deciding how to present the club most attractively.

Reasons for choice of club amongst 15–19-year-olds

	%
Friendly atmosphere/friends there	55
Near my home	45
Value for money	33
Well-run	32
Playing facilities not too overcrowded	17
High standard of facilities	32
Caters for children	7
Licensed bar	17
Good reputation/standard of play	17
Professional advice and/or coaching	19
Car parking	4
Refreshments	6
Don't know	4

Source: Mintel

 Assignment 9

Go to your local sports club and find out how it is managed. You may be able to obtain a brochure about it and a copy of the rules. One of the officials may be willing to explain how the committees work, and how the club raises its money and determines subscription rates. He or she may be willing to talk to your whole group.

Look at the facilities offered for the fees charged. Try to decide if it is a happy club or not. If members of your group are able to find out about a variety of local sports clubs you will be able to discuss in detail their strengths and weaknesses given the particular activity with which each is involved.

Working in a sports centre

AIMS

To gain knowledge and understanding of:

- employment opportunities available in the sport and leisure industries
- the organisation and administration of a large sport and leisure centre

To develop the skills of:

- reception duties including financial calculations
- sports competition administration
- research, analysis and presentation of sport-related information
- conducting a survey

Working in sport

Sport-related employment is the sixth largest area of employment in the UK, accounting for 376,000 workers.

Obviously, few of the people employed in this area are involved in professional sport as a career but in one way or another they help to keep the sport and leisure industry thriving. For instance, there are currently 1,500 sport and leisure centres in the UK employing some 40–50,000 people. The following section looks at one such centre in detail.

Picketts Lock Leisure Centre

Picketts Lock is situated 10 miles from central London and is close to the M11, M25 and A406 North Circular Road. It is part of the Lee Valley Leisure Park which combines sport with the natural environment. The park is being developed by the Lee Valley Regional Park Authority which was established in 1967. Further details are available in *Sport Examined* (P. Beashel and J. Taylor, 1986, Macmillan).

Sporting activities catered for at the centre include the following:

Swimming

Squash

Badminton

Table tennis

Sauna

Fitness

Rifle shooting

Roller skating

Snooker

Tennis

Bowls

Trampoline

Circuit training

Archery

Soccer

Hockey

Golf

Camping

Gymnastics

Putting

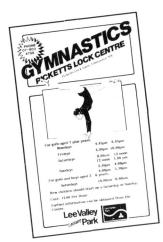

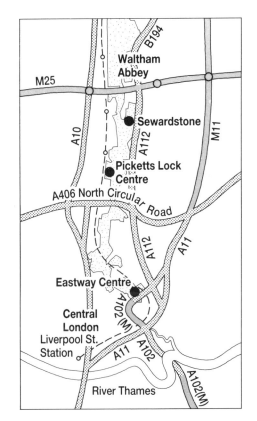

The centre also acts as a focal point for many other large-scale activities. These include:

Dog shows	Exhibitions (various)
Cat shows	Car boot sales
Budgie shows	Indoor sales
Entomological shows	Fashion shows
London Championship	Weddings
Show (rodents)	Engagements
Bowls tournaments	Anniversaries
Darts tournaments	Concerts
Fireworks	Parties
Dinghy shows	Conferences
Antique bazaars	Seminars
Craft fairs	

Assignment 1

Picketts Lock Sports and Leisure had takings in
excess of £900,000 for the year April 1986–March
1987.

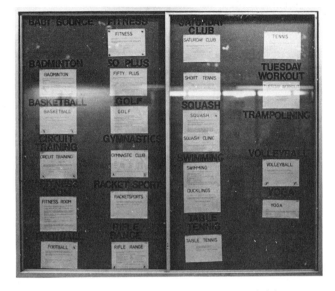

The number of participants in various activities
included:

Swimming	111,157	Gym/clubroom	21,966
Sauna	7,088	Crèche	4,555
Solarium	1,492	Bowls hall	68,870
Squash	44,939		
Sports hall		**Great hall**	
Five-a-side	1,861	General hire	83,184
Badminton	39,836	Cat/dog shows	30,850
Hire	12,319	Snooker	12,070
Courses–sessions	30,359	Angling	26
Holiday activities	10,108	School usage	18,339
		Camping	32,268
Fitness room	13,167	Fireworks	9,000
Conference room	626	Golf driving-range	41,929

Use the participation numbers given in order to
carry out the following:

1 Construct a bar chart to compare the numbers
using the following facilities. Round the figures up
or down to the nearest thousand. The first two are
done for you.

Swimming	111,000	Fitness room	
Sauna	7,000	Crèche	
Solarium		Bowls hall	
Squash		Great hall	
Sports hall		Snooker	
Gym/clubroom		Golf driving-range	

2 Construct a pie chart to compare the numbers of
participants in the following sports:

Swimming
Badminton
Fitness
Snooker
Golf driving-range
Five-a-side football

3 Calculate the school usage as a percentage of
overall usage of the centre.

 Assignment 2

Staffing

Over 100 full- and part-time staff are employed to
keep the centre working efficiently. It is vital that
each individual member of staff has a specific job
description so that they:

(a) Know what they are expected to do
(b) Know to whom they are accountable
(c) Know for whom they have responsibility

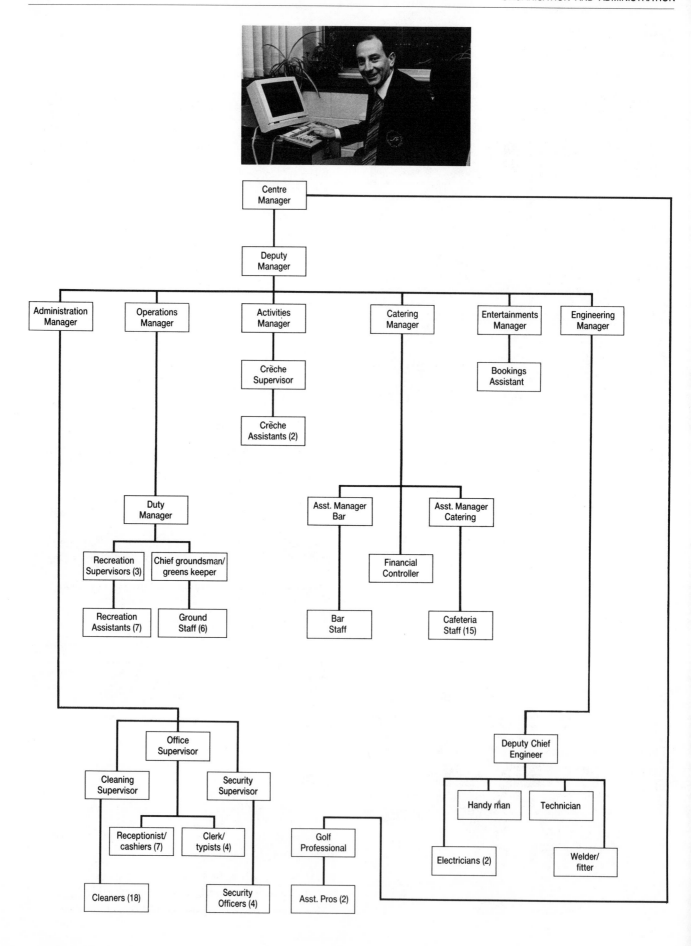

Sample job descriptions

Cashier/receptionists

- Handling cash, cheques and credit cards for payment of general sports equipment and activities.
- Taking daily payments through the post for various sports and entertainments.
- Taking and recording golf range money.
- Taking and recording payment for schools.
- Taking Barclaycard and Access bookings for Sailing Centre in the evenings and at weekends.
- Taking telephone bookings for sports one week in advance.
- Controlling switchboard, answering general telephone enquiries and taking messages.
- Daily processing and filing of membership applications.
- Monthly filing and updates of memberships and despatching monthly renewal letters.
- Issuing weekly wage slips.
- Issuing of sports hire.
- Control of lighting.
- Giving out change for refreshment machines.
- Taking course money and issuing cards.
- Processing of fitness room cards.

Activities assistant/clerk typist

- General activities: typing and enquiries; helping organise course leaflets; ensuring equipment is provided for all coaching courses and sessions; making out course register sheets; liaising with coaching staff regarding the running of courses.
- Helping organise staff for birthday parties.
- Ensuring minimum numbers are reached on courses and cancelling where necessary.
- Organising and running the squash leagues and helping with competitions.
- Helping with the organisation of football league.
- Helping the Entertainments Department for one day per week.
- Typing bookings memos regarding set-up requirements.
- Dealing with all bookings and enquiries for Sailing Centre, in person, mail and telephone.
- Processing all payments for courses related to the Sailing Centre.
- Forwarding sailing course information to the general public.
- Informing reception and Sailing Centre of course booking situations.
- Keeping all records of bookings and payments regarding Sailing Centre.

Working as a group and using the job descriptions above as a guide, compose job descriptions for the following positions:

(a) Groundsman/greenkeeper
(b) Activities manager
(c) Centre manager

Assignment 3

You are a cashier/receptionist at a large sports centre and are on duty at a very busy time of the day. You receive a rapid series of telephone calls and reception requests as well as requests from the centre as soon as you start on duty. Deal with the following situations either by supplying the information yourself or by referring the caller to the appropriate member of staff.

| T = Telephone, R = Reception, I = Internal |

R: One to use solarium for one hour.
R: Boy from badminton lesson with bleeding finger.
T: Request for information on short tennis (as full as possible).
T: Family of four want to camp at the centre for four nights (motor caravan) and they also want an external hook-up.
I: Report that the date on the fire extinguishers has expired.
R: Four to play badminton for one hour.
T: Family of two children plus three adults for skating (early).
R: Man in to renew his family membership.
R: Two unemployed persons to play squash for 45 minutes.
T: 12-year-old wants to know details of any squash courses.
R: Woman representing the Great Antique Road Show wishes to make a booking for the Great Hall next April.
T: Tennis court booking for next Monday.
I: Part-time cleaner pops in to collect her wages.

Copy and complete the Action Sheet below in order to indicate the action you have taken. The first two situations have been completed for you.

SITUATION	ACTION TAKEN
1 Solarium	Cost 2.50/hour. Took money, issued ticket and change.
2 Boy with bleeding finger	Contacted duty officer to apply first aid.

You will need to make appropriate use of the extracts from the Activities Price List given below.

ACTIVITIES		PRICE £	ACTIVITIES		PRICE £
Swimming	Adult	0.65	Squash	30 Mins Peak Hours	2.20
	Child	0.45		45 Mins Peak Hours	3.30
	OAP and disabled	0.45		60 Mins Peak Hours	4.40
				30 Mins Off-Peak Hours	1.60
				45 Mins Off-Peak Hours	2.40
				60 Mins Off-Peak Hours	3.20
				Saturday Squash Members	1.10
				Under 16. 30 Mins Off-Peak	1.60

ACTIVITIES		PRICE £
Badminton	60 Mins Peak Hours	3.80
	60 Mins Off-Peak Hours	3.00
	30 Mins Peak Hours	1.90
	30 Mins Off-Peak Hours	1.50
	Saturday Badminton Members	1.50
	Under 16. 60 Mins Off-Peak	2.20
Sauna	Individual	2.80
	Solarium	2.50
	Sauna/Massage	5.00
	Family Sauna	6.00
	Sauna/Solarium	4.50
Fitness room	Off-Peak	1.30
	Peak	1.70
Roller skating	Late Skate (Peak). Member	1.25
	Early Skate (Off-Peak). Child Member	1.10
	Early Skate. Adult Member	1.10
	Late Skate. Adult Non-Member	1.45
	Early Skate. Child Non-Member	1.20
	Early Skate. Adult Non-Member	1.20
	Skate Hire	0.40
	Junior Skate	0.55
Tennis	60 Mins	3.25
Crèche	120 Mins	1.20
	60 Mins	0.60

SESSIONS

RECREATION

Short tennis	120 Mins	1.50
Roller hockey	120 Mins	1.00
50 plus	120 Mins	0.80
Circuit training	120 Mins	1.25
Putting green	Per Round (18 Holes)	0.60

CAMPING Note: touring site only

CAR/MOTORCARAVAN

Caravan/tent including 2 persons	Per Night	4.50
Backpacker	Per Night	2.00
Additional persons	Per Night	1.00
Electrical hook-up	Per Night	1.50

MEMBERSHIPS		£
Memberships	Family	19.50
	Family Renewal	17.00
	Adult	14.00
	Adult Renewal	12.00
	Youth	7.00
	Youth Renewal	6.00
	Student	7.00
	Student Renewal	6.00
	Off Peak	7.00
	Off Peak Renewal	6.00
	OAP	7.00
	OAP Renewal	6.00
	Crèche	1.00

UNEMPLOYED

Rates		
	Centre Entry	0.20
	Swimming Pool	0.40
	Badminton	1.55
	Squash 45 Mins	1.65
	Squash 30 Mins	1.10
	Table Tennis	0.65

COURSES

Short tennis	1 Hour every Saturday for 6 weeks	6.00 Total cost
Squash	45 Mins every Friday for 6 weeks. 10–14 year olds	7.50 Total cost

HIRING

Facilities available for hire		Usage
	Bowls Hall	Bowling External Exams Badminton
	Great Hall	Weddings Cat/Dog shows Concerts Fashion shows Exhibitions
	Gym	Gymnastics Martial Arts
	Rifle Range	Pistols Rifles Archery
	Club Rooms	Martial Arts
	Top Deck	Special Occasions

Assignment 4

You are an assistant to the activities manager and have been given the following tasks to complete as soon as possible:

1 Prepare a leaflet advertising a women's body-toning course which will take place on every Friday for 12 weeks starting in six weeks' time. The cost of the course will be £15.00.

2 The squash league secretary has recently had a car accident and you now discover that he has not yet organised the club's senior knock-out competition. All you have is a list of the names of the players and their club rankings. Draw up a chart to ensure that the top four seeds do not meet until the semi-finals nor the top two seeds until the final.

Tim	5	Paul	
Jack		John	
Andy	8	Fred	3
Harry	7	Bruce	1
Bill		Jerry	
Chris	2	David	
Peter	4	George	
Geoff		Tony	6

3 The football season is about to start and you have to prepare the Christmas result sheet to show how the 12 teams are getting on. Three points are awarded for a win, one for a draw and none for a loss. In the case of an equal number of points the team with the better goal difference is the winner.

4 A tennis doubles knock-out competition which you set up for the centre players has reached the final eight. The competition is due to finish by the end of next week but you have just heard that recent flooding has damaged all but one of the tennis courts.

You can make use of the one remaining tennis court for one afternoon session and the evening session on each of the following days next week:

Monday, Wednesday, Friday and Saturday.

You have contacted all of the players concerned and each has stated the times that they can play.

Pair of players	Afternoon or evening	Suitable days
Mr Sabido & Miss Nomer	Afternoon only	Sat
Mr Hicks & Mrs Collins	Afternoon or evening	Wed
Mr Beashel & Mrs Beashel	Afternoon or evening	Sat
Miss Keith & Mr Black	Evening only	Mon
Mr Stratford & Miss Ever	Evening only	Wed
Mr Taylor & Mrs Taylor	Afternoon only	Fri
Mr Goodnight & Miss Bye	Afternoon or evening	Mon
Miss Take & Mr Green	Afternoon or evening	Fri

Plan the programme of games for the week.

Assignment 5

You are activities manager and have just received the letter opposite referring to a children's holiday course which you ran during the recent school holidays. Make use of the price list on pages 20 and 21 in order to send a reply to the woman in question.

Assignment 6

You are the manager of a small sports centre in the West Midlands. You have a full-time staff of six and a part-time staff of eight.

The task

Working as a group prepare a short report outlining the action you would take in the following circumstances. Read through all of the cases but be ready to give your solutions to the two cases which will be allocated to you. You have 20 minutes to prepare a response. Choose the person to record and report back for your group. Consider the implications of your decisions. If you complete your two cases before the time is up then work on another case. At the end of 20 minutes a spokesperson will be expected to report back for each group.

The Mansion
Yessex
8th. November

Dear Sir or Madam,

I am writing to express my anger at the way my 14 year old son, Wayne, was treated at the recent Activities course which you held at the centre.

The brochure advertising the course offered a number of activities, including fitness training. You can imagine my son's disappointment when he was told that it was not possible to offer that part of the course because only he had opted to do it.

He had to take part in squash, tennis, badminton and roller skating instead, and although he did not complain to me about it, I know that he was most upset. Can you tell me why you did not keep your word?

I would also like to know why the cost of the course was so high. Wayne is a member of the centre, and yet he had to pay £20.00 for two days (24 hours) of the four activities which he was forced to take part in. Surely it would have been cheaper for him just to go to the Centre for four days and pay separately for each of the activities, even if he went at peak times?

I am looking forward to a speedy reply to this letter. I may well write to my local M.P. Mr Charles Raynesford (Conservative) if your reply is unsatisfactory.

Yours faithfully,

Penelope Pemberton~Smythe

The cases

1   The senior receptionist informs you that she suspects an assistant receptionist of fraud. The assistant has only been at the centre for a short period of time and has always appeared to you to be very helpful and keen to learn. The senior receptionist believes that the girl is letting her friends in without paying. She also heard a customer complaining that she had not been given all of her change.

2   Despite repeated warnings the appearance of one of the full-time members of staff is persistently scruffy and he is off-hand to customers. He has been at the centre for a long time and has lost his original enthusiasm. He is very good with the disabled group who use the centre however, and you would find it hard to get someone to take over his role with the disabled swimmers.

3   The fire brigade visited the centre recently to inspect the fire alarm systems and watch a fire drill. Their report expressed dissatisfaction with the speed at which the public left the centre. One member of staff actually kept his swimming class in the centre. When questioned by the fire brigade he said he knew 'it was only a drill'.

4   You receive yet another report of new graffiti in the ladies' toilet. It was first spotted after the local comprehensive school was at the centre. The last time that you complained to the school about problems with their pupils the teacher in charge argued strongly that it could not possibly be her pupils because they had been told to be on their best behaviour and they would not let her down.

5   A mother has made a complaint that her 14-year-old daughter is being supported too enthusiastically by the part-time gymnastics teacher, a 24-year-old married man. He has been coaching at the centre for the last six months after moving into the area from the north of England. This is the first complaint you have received against him.

6   The local swimming club, which is very strong, uses the centre swimming pool on two nights a week. They have reached the National Swimming Club finals and have requested another two nights a week for training. One of the nights they have requested is currently being used by a local youth centre and the other night is taken up by a group for the handicapped.

Assignment 7

Organise a survey of your own local sports and leisure centre. Be sure to ask the manager for his permission and help before you start. Try to include the following in your survey:

- **(a)** Name and situation of centre
- **(b)** Facilities
- **(c)** Activities
- **(d)** Staffing
- **(e)** Special activities
- **(f)** Pricing
- **(g)** Finance

Be sure to present your findings in the most effective way. Consult the appendices for guidance.

 Assignment 8

Perhaps you feel that working in one capacity or another in a sport and leisure centre would be for you. Find out what qualifications and training you need.

Write a letter requesting details to one or more of the following associations, who should be able to provide you with up-to-date information.

Also see if you can obtain copies of some of the journals and papers published by these and other associations involved in the sport and leisure industry. These include the following:

The Leisure Manager, a journal published by The Institute of Leisure and Amenity Management

Sports Industry, a journal for sports and leisure managers

Sport and Leisure, the magazine of the Sports Council

There are many more specialist magazines which could contain useful background information for you. Look in your library and ask your local sports centre manager for help.

Investigate the possibility of doing some work experience or work-shadowing in a sport or leisure centre. If your school or college is involved in work experience already then your task should be straightforward. If not then talk to the person responsible for careers and tell him where your interests lie.

Finally don't forget to contact your local careers office. Invite an officer into your school or college in order to talk about careers in sport.

Institute of Baths and Recreation Management
Gifford House
36–38 Gifford House
Melton Mowbray
Leicestershire LE13 1XJ

Institute of Leisure and Amenity Management
Lower Basildon
Reading
Berkshire RG8 9NE

The Sports Council
16 Upper Woburn Place
London
WC1H 0QP

The Grapefruit Health and Fitness Club

AIMS

To gain knowledge and understanding of:

- opportunities for employment in the health and fitness industry
- health and fitness attitudes
- sports fitness and participation levels
- why people join sports clubs
- job descriptions in the health and fitness area

To develop the skills of:

- assessing individual fitness levels
- planning programmes of health and fitness activities
- oral presentation
- decision-making
- administration
- writing effectively for a specific audience

Large numbers of people in this country have begun to realise that the quality of their lives is improved if they can maintain a reasonable degree of fitness. In an attempt to become and stay fit many have sought out health and fitness clubs. New clubs have sprung up all over the country. Some are run by the local authority but many are private and run very much as a business.

 Assignment 1

Imagine that you are an assistant manager of a privately run fitness club on the south coast. You recently applied for a manager's post in a brand-new fitness club in the north of England. After a very good interview you were offered and accepted the post.

Respond to the following correspondence from the director of the health and fitness club for which you are going to work.

The Grapefruit Health and Fitness Club,
Heathland Road,
Heathlake,
Yorkshire

25th January 1988

Dear Colleague,

THE GRAPEFRUIT HEALTH AND FITNESS CLUB

Congratulations on your appointment as Manager of the new Grapefruit Health
and Fitness Club. I am sure that the club will develop to its full
potential under your guidance and control.

As you are aware the club is due to open in 3 month's time, although you
join the company at the end of this month. The building is going according
to schedule and your two full-time assistants have been appointed.

I have enclosed the following information in order to assist you to
complete the assignments which you agreed to undertake at the time of
your interview:

1 A copy of the Market Research commissioned by us and conducted by
Jupta.

2 Some profiles of a number of local people who were interviewed by Jupta
and who indicated that they would be joining the club as soon as it opens.

3 Copies of advertising leaflets distributed by the one other health and
fitness club near us.

I have also attached the assignments in order to refresh your memory.

Finally you must remember that the costs of the Grapefruit Club have so
far been met by the shareholders. It will have to start paying its way
in the very near future. The shareholders are confident that you are
the best person for the job and we look forward to many years of
profit sharing with you.

I look forward to hearing from you in the next couple of weeks.

Yours in Sport,

JAMES CATHCART,

Company Director of the Grapefruit Health and Fitness Club.

Plan of Grapefruit Health and Fitness Club

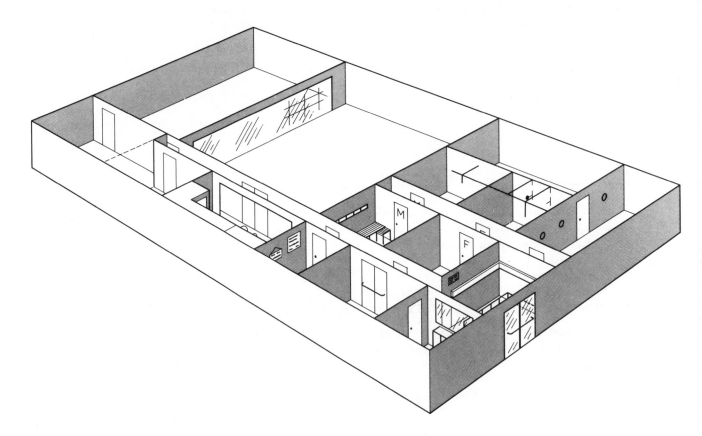

Summary of market research carried out on behalf of The Grapefruit Health and Fitness Club

This summary report contains information on national trends in the health and fitness field as well as a more detailed breakdown of the market potential in the area of Heathlake, Yorkshire.

The last ten years have witnessed a dramatic growth in the general public's awareness of the need to stay healthy through a combination of sound eating habits and regular exercise. A national survey conducted by The Health Education Council in 1983 indicated this growth.

Attitudes to own health 1983

	%
Very healthy	32
Reasonably healthy but could do better	51
Unhealthy	8
Don't know	9

Source: Health Education Council/Consumers Association

If almost 60% of the population agree that they could be fitter, then the health and fitness industry has a very large market available to it.

These attitudes do not translate into active participation levels however. Very small numbers of the general population take part in sport and/or fitness activities on a regular basis.

Research by Mintel based on a nationally represented sample of 1399 adults indicated the following participation trends. (Regular visits defined as 'once a week or more').

Regularly visit a gymnasium or regularly participate in classes

Type of person	Gymnasium %	Classes
All	8	6
Men	12	5
Women	5	7
Housewives	4	6
Other women	10	17
Age		
15–19	20	13
20–24	7	7
25–34	14	7
35–44	9	8
45–54	6	6
55–64	7	5
65 +	*	2

*denotes less than 1%   Source: Mintel.

Mintel also found that private clubs are facing an increasing challenge in the market from local authority provision because of the subsidised nature of their pricing and also by the improving quality of their facilities.

Jupta also carried out a social survey in the Heathlake locality. A brief summary of their conclusions is shown below.

Summary of survey carried out in Heathlake for The Grapefruit Health and Fitness Club

Population	197,000.
Communications	Excellent motorway links to all areas to north, south, east and west.
Business/commerce	Old steel works which used to be the single largest employer has recently closed with large numbers being made redundant. The town has been classified as an enterprise zone and a number of small but successful Hi-Tech companies have moved into the town's new industrial estate.
Schools/colleges	Number of well-equipped schools in the area. A city technology college has recently been established in new buildings. The local authority believes in 'dual use' and most of the schools have good sports facilities.
Competition	One other health and fitness club situated some miles from the Grapefruit site. Appears to be doing quite well but limits its activities to aerobics and dance-type fitness sessions. Membership is £250 per year which includes the use of all facilities and a limited number of 'free' classes.

As in the national surveys the people of Heathlake show a realistic awareness of their levels of health and fitness.

Attitudes to own health

Base 500 adults	%
Very healthy	36
Reasonably healthy but could do better	46
Unhealthy	11
Don't know	7

Source: Jupta.

Once again however the vast majority do nothing positive in order to become fitter and healthier.

Participation in sporting activities in last month

Base 500 adults

	Outdoor %	Indoor %
Males	32	36
Females	17	21

Source: Jupta.

Jupta also attempted to find out which particular sporting activities were pursued by those who decided to become more active.

Those who have taken up sporting activities in the last 2 years for health and fitness reasons

Base 500 adults	%
All	22
Swimming	8
Jogging	7
Keep fit/aerobics/dance class	4
Gym/weights/circuits	3
Cycling	2
Badminton	3
Bowls	4
Squash	1
Other sports	3
None/Don't know	63

Source: Jupta.

A most revealing section of the survey sought to establish why present sports club members actually decide to join clubs. The results are shown below and should be of great help to the new management of the Grapefruit Health and Fitness Club.

Reasons why people choose a specific sports/health club

	%
Friendly atmosphere-friends there	47
Near home	35
Good value for money	33
Well run	26
Not too overcrowded	21
High standard of facilities	20
Caters for children	20
Licensed/health bar	25
Good reputation	13
Professional advice/coaching	12
Car parking	8
Refreshments	6
Don't know	12

Source: Jupta.

Assignment 2

Taking into account the facilities and equipment (as shown on the plan of the club) as well as the Jupta findings, produce the following:

1 A one-week programme of activities showing clearly what you intend to offer, whom the courses are aimed at and when they will take place.

2 Copy out the plan of the club and indicate where the following facilities will be sited:

Reception	Fitness room
Bar	Multi-gym
Bar store	Health bar
Staff room	Facial beauty room
Office	Changing rooms
First aid room	Showers
Sauna	Whirlpool
Solarium	Toilets
Dance studio	Crèche

You may be able to think of other attractions to include in the centre but you must remember that you need to get a good return on any money that you spend.

You may also like to decide how the Grapefruit Health and Fitness Club should be decorated. Decide upon the most suitable colour schemes for each particular part of the building.

Assignment 3

Please prepare the following for the Board to consider:

1 A publicity leaflet which can be distributed to all households in the area. Remember, unless you can attract members then the club will never be successful. Below is an example of our competitor's publicity.

2 A 30-second commercial to go on to the local community radio. This will be very expensive so make sure the message is really punchy.

3 A logo which can be put on to all written material issued by the club.

Assignment 4

Describe the three tests you intend to use in order to assess the fitness levels of our customers.

The tests should:

(a) be simple to administer
(b) be safe to undertake
(c) be enjoyable for the customer
(d) include a measure of the customer's strength, suppleness and stamina

After a hard day at the office or at home with the kids, what you need is some gentle exercise designed to make you feel full of life again. Our aerobics and dance classes can make your body into the best type of

busy body

... one ready to take on the world once more ... one full of life and energy ... a body you feel proud of ... one with the shape you desire and the weight you long to achieve ... get your new body at

Busy Body

Sample of a competitor's publicity material.

Assignment 5

Below are profiles of four of the residents who expressed a strong desire to join the new club. Read the profiles carefully and then write letters to them suggesting what the club will be able to offer them when it opens.

1 Enid Blyth

56-year-old widow, recently retired on a good pension. Has always maintained a good level of fitness. Walks at least three miles every day and plays tennis twice a week in the summer. Wants to join the aerobics lessons as well as use the sauna and solarium.

2 Kevin Trickett

19 years old, single, unemployed since leaving school. Played a lot of football at school and still considers himself fit despite the fact that he does little exercise at the moment. Is hoping to join the club in order to increase his overall body strength.

3 Dennis Bruce

40 years old, a plumber who is married with two teenage children. Exercise limited to walking the dog, cleaning the car and the occasional game of golf. Remembers his days as a sprinter of some repute. Keen to join the club as he wants to lose a few pounds and also become fitter than his golfing partners.

4 Rachel Gibson

31 years old, married with four-year-old daughter. Works as a computer programmer in the Heathlake industrial estate. Was once an active sportsperson but now out of shape and overweight. Wishes to regain her former sylph-like figure.

 # Assignment 6

A number of part-time assistants will need to be employed at the club at different times of the week. Please draw up a job description and also give your opinion on the type of person who would be most suitable in terms of personality and ability. (See page 19 for example of a job description.)

Sport for all

AIMS

AIMS

To gain knowledge and understanding of:

- the sporting needs of the disabled
- the ways in which buildings can be modified to help the disabled
- sporting opportunities available to the disabled
- the benefits of being involved with the sporting disabled

To develop the skills of:

- formulating a questionnaire
- detailed surveys
- investigation
- written and oral communication
- obtaining information from a variety of sources

Sport for all?

Sport is not just for the able-bodied. As the photographs here show, people with a variety of disabilities can gain great excitement, pleasure and achievement from sporting activities.

It is still difficult for many disabled people to take part in sport. Although it has been accepted that sports buildings should be designed to allow disabled people full access to, and use of, all facilities, many buildings currently in use cause frustration and disabled people therefore tend not to use them, simply because of their design.

We need to look at the needs of five major groups of disabled people in order that they can be catered for effectively.

These groups are:

1 Wheelchair users – these people depend on their wheelchairs for their mobility. Some are independent whilst others are totally dependent on a helper. Wheelchair users are at a particular disadvantage because they:

- (i) are at a lower level than anyone else
- (ii) are wider than anyone else
- (iii) are able to go only where their wheels will take them

2 Ambulant disabled – disabled people who are able to walk but may depend on **prostheses** (artificial limbs), **orthoses** (calipers), sticks, crutches or walking aids. Also included are those who may have some physical disability which affects their mobility e.g. people with heart complaints who cannot over-exert themselves.

3 Deaf and hard-of-hearing – this disability is often not recognised by the general public and sufferers may be thought of as being slow, simple-minded or rude. Fortunately most sports depend on vision and physical ability so the hard-of-hearing and deaf may get full enjoyment from sport.

4 Visually handicapped – this includes people who are totally blind or partially sighted or who have visual imperfections such as colour blindness which makes visual cues difficult to interpret.

5 Mentally handicapped – the range of mental handicap can vary enormously, the most severe being affected with physical handicap as well.

We should not forget the needs of the temporarily disabled. Physiotherapy and closely-monitored physical activities can be valuable for people recovering from injuries of all sorts.

![] Assignment 1

As a group find out as much as you can about disabled sports groups in your area. Work in pairs, each pair to investigate a different category of disability. See if you can visit a club session. Talk to the participants and find out the practical problems of the disabled sportsperson. Report back to your **group within 2 weeks.**

 **Assignment 2**

A prominent member of the local Sports Council recently retired through ill health. You have been co-opted in her place. She had always been concerned for the needs of the sporting disabled and had started to draw up a sports centre checklist designed to see how sporting establishments catered for the needs of the disabled sportsperson.

You have been asked to complete this task. The partly completed checklist is shown below. As you can see one or two sections have been fully researched whilst others are very sketchy.

Sport for the Disabled – Sports Centre Checklist

Sports Centre Name ....

Centre Manager ....

Date survey was carried out:..

Area	Main Points	Yes	No	Recommended Improvements
Access	Is it easy to get to the centre?	☐	☐	
	Is the entrance safe, flat, well lit, at least 2m wide with clearly contrasting edges, provided with handrails and with seats at regular intervals?	☐	☐	
	Is the pavement at the same level as the road surface?	☐	☐	
	If the entrance is raised, is there both a ramp and steps leading to it?	☐	☐	
	Is it free from potential obstacles such as lamp posts or benches set back from the footpaths?	☐	☐	
Entrance	Is the entrance common to all users and protected from the weather?	☐	☐	
Signs	?	☐	☐	
Telephones	?	☐	☐	
Assistance	?	☐	☐	
Communication	Is information given by loudspeaker announcements?	☐	☐	
	By visual display panels?	☐	☐	
	Is there an audible alarm?	☐	☐	

Corridors	Are the corridors at least 1.2m wide?	☐ ☐	
	Do they have non-resistant floors?	☐ ☐	
	Are they well-lit?	☐ ☐	
	Do they have hand-rails?	☐ ☐	
Doors	?	☐ ☐	
Lifts	?	☐ ☐	
Changing rooms	Are the wash basins set at different levels?	☐ ☐	
	Can the hair dryers be used by wheelchair sportsmen and women?	☐ ☐	
	Does the toilet / shower area have slip-resistant floors?	☐ ☐	
	Is this area level?	☐ ☐	
Social areas	Are the restaurants, snack bars and licensed bar accessible to wheelchair users?	☐ ☐	
	Are the aisles between rows of tables wide enough for wheelchairs (0.8m)?	☐ ☐	
Spectating areas	Does the design of these areas take account of the lower eye level of people in wheelchairs and of children?	☐ ☐	
Guide dogs		☐ ☐	
General	Does the sports centre integrate the disabled sportsperson into its teams and competitions?	☐ ☐	
	Does it do any more than simply providing help at disabled events?	☐ ☐	

 Assignment 3

Using your checklist, or a modified version of it, survey your local sports centre.

Find out which particular sporting activities are provided for the disabled and the number of disabled people attending the centre.

Contact the manager before you visit and ask for permission to carry out the survey. Promise to give him or her a copy of the results.

 Assignment 4

Draw up a number of proposals which would help to make the sports centre even more helpful for the disabled. Remember it is often the small, simple and cheap modifications that provide the most benefits to the largest number of people. Also remember that improvements for the disabled are often improvements for all users.

Assignment 5

Even if the local sports centre makes special provision for disabled sportspersons, there may still be problems of finance to overcome. A wheelchair suitable for sport costs over £1,000 and can be as much as £5,000. Carry out a survey in order to find out how local disabled sportspersons overcome the financial problems of taking part in sport. Investigate such matters as the costs of joining clubs, transport, entrance fees and sponsorship.

 Assignment 6

Swimming pool survey

Many disabled people only fully experience the joy of unrestricted movement without help when in water. For this reason it is vital that every opportunity should be taken to ensure that swimming pool time for the disabled is available.

Although most swimming pools have set times for swimming clubs and for the disabled, the individual disabled person should be made welcome at any sessions open to the general public.

It is wise for the disabled swimmer to be accompanied on a one-to-one basis even if they are very good swimmers, to ensure that they are not impeded by unaware members of the general public.

Carry out an investigation in order to find out if it is easy for the disabled person to use your local pool. You will find that many of the points made earlier will be applicable but there are also some problems which are unique to swimming.

You will need to prepare a checklist of questions **which you can ask at your local swimming pool.**

Work in groups of three or four to see how many different questions you can think of. When you have exhausted your efforts look at the checklist opposite and compare your results with a completed checklist.

 Assignment 7

We have looked in some detail at the sports provision for the disabled at sports centres and swimming pools, but this is far from the whole story. Almost every sport, from hang-gliding to climbing, has disabled people taking part. Select your particular sporting activity and find out how disabled people take part.

You should also find out about the many specialist sporting associations such as The British Society of One-Arm Golfers and the Phab associations. Try your local Sports Council for names and addresses of these clubs.

 Assignment 8

Competition is an in-built part of most sports, whether you are competing as an individual, in a team or merely against yourself. But how easy is it for the disabled to compete in their particular sport?

1   Find out the following about the paraplegic games:

   (a) where and when they take place
   (b) how many people take part
   (c) what sporting events they contain
   (d) any other relevant information

2   Discover what sporting competitions are organised for the mentally disabled both nationally as well as in your own locality.

3   Finally, see if you can visit some sporting sessions for the disabled. You may want to stay and help on a regular basis.

Swimming pool survey: checklist

	Yes	No	Recommended Improvements

1. Are all of the following on the same level: entrance;

changing area;

pre-cleanse area;

pool;

refreshment area;

viewing gallery?

2. If some of the above are at different levels, is it still possible for a disabled person to get to all parts of the building?

3. Is there at least one family (unisex) changing room in order that the swimmer may be assisted by a relative or friend?

4. If there is a central clothes storage centre, is it as close as possible to the changing area?

5. If lockers are provided can they be readily used by a disabled person?

6. Are there a number of large lockers in which crutches or calipers may be stored?

7. Are the showers and toilet areas an integral part of the changing rooms?

8. Are the changing rooms as close as possible to the poolside?

9. Are there hand-rails between the pre-cleanse area and the poolside?

10. Are skeleton wheelchairs or trolleys with a back rest available in order to transport disabled to poolside?

11. If footbaths are provided, is there a short by-pass route so that the disabled person need not change level?

12. Is the entry to the poolside at the shallow end? (This is particularly important for the visually and mentally handicapped.)

13. Is the pool surround at least 2 metres wide?

14. Is entry to the pool possible by means of a recessed staircase with hand-rails on both sides?

15. Are the following available to assist entry: portable steps with handrails at both sides;

slides;

shutes;

soft mat to sit on;

hydraulically or mechanically operated hoists;

any other poolside aids?

16. Does the water come flush with the deck level or is it below the poolside?

17. Is the water temperature adequate (27–32°C)?

18. Does the pool run from shallow end to deep end at a steady incline (1:28)?

19. Is the floor surface rough enough to give a grip but smooth enough not to hurt sensitive skin?

20. Are heated seats provided at the poolside?

Blowing the whistle

AIMS

To gain knowledge and understanding of:

- the need for rules and regulations in sporting events
- the role of officials in sport
- the rules of a wide variety of sporting activities
- sports terminology

To develop the skills of:

- sports administration
- collecting information
- matching information

Taking part in sporting events can be exciting, exhilarating, taxing and frustrating. For many of us, taking part is the most important thing, whether we actually win or lose is not important. Many sports are competitive however, and although we may get pleasure from a well-executed shot or an effective tackle, we get even more pleasure from being a member of a winning team or the individual winner of a competition.

It is possible to play some competitive games without the assistance of referees, umpires, or other officials, although most sporting events do require the presence of one or more official. At national and international events, it is amazing how many officials are required to make the proceedings run smoothly. For example, the minimum number of officials for an international swimming match is as follows: a referee, a starter, a chief timekeeper, three timekeepers per lane plus two reserve timekeepers, a chief judge, three finishing judges per lane, two inspectors of turn per lane (one at each end), two judges of stroke, a clerk of the course, a recorder and an announcer.

Announcing

Athletics meeting between

ROCHTON ATHLETIC CLUB

and

EXTON TERRIERS

SATURDAY 12th JUNE at 2.00 p.m.

at

ROCHTON ATHLETICS TRACK

Spectators welcome

Refreshments

 ## Assignment 1

As fixture secretary of Rochton Athletics Club you have been asked to organise the officials for your next league match. The following events are to be included.

sprints	mid/long distance	relays	hurdles	throws	jumps
100m 200m 400m	800m 1500m 5000m	4 × 100 4 × 400	100m (w) 110m (m) 400m steeplechase (m)	javelin discus shot hammer (m)	high long triple (m) pole vault (m)

There will be events for men and women except where indicated above

Draw up the list of officials you would need to supervise this match. State the responsibilities of each official.

 ## Assignment 2

Few sporting events need the number of officials necessary to organise an athletics or swimming match, but most need more than one.

Copy out and complete the table opposite which indicates the particular officials necessary to run different sporting events.

Sport	Officials
Synchronised swimming	....
Rugby union	....
Cricket	....
....	First referee, second referee, 4 linesmen, a score pad operator and a visual score operator.

Assignment 3

One of the many responsibilities assigned to officials is to ensure that the correct number of players takes part in team games. They are also responsible for ensuring that the rules regarding substitution are not violated.

Place the following sports in the correct place in the chart opposite.

Water polo
Rugby union
Baseball
Soccer
Basketball

Australian rules football
Lacrosse (men's)
Volleyball
Football (Canadian)

Sport	Number of players	Number of subs
?	5	5
?	6	6
?	7	4
?	9	any number
?	10	9
?	11	2
?	12	any number
?	15	2 for injury
?	18	2

 Assignment 4

The officials also have to ensure that games are scored properly and that they finish in the proper manner. Some sporting events take place over a specified period of time whilst others are played until an individual or team wins the necessary number of sets or innings.

Match the following sports with the appropriate duration.

Shinty
Test cricket
Handball (team)
Field hockey
Gaelic football

Korfball
American football
Netball
Polo
Rugby league

Sport	Duration
?	two halves of 45 minutes
?	two halves of 35 minutes
?	five days each of six hours' duration
?	four quarters of 15 minutes (playing time)
?	six chukkas of 7 minutes
?	two periods of 30 minutes
?	four periods of 15 minutes
?	two periods of 30 minutes
?	two halves of 20 minutes (playing time)
?	two halves of 40 minutes

 Assignment 5

When individuals or teams are evenly matched it is sometimes difficult to get a result in the designated time. In cup or knock-out competitions a result is necessary. The governing bodies of each of the following sports have developed ways of ensuring that one team or individual eventually wins without the game going on forever. Describe how each of them has designed their rules or laws to achieve this end.

Tennis
High jump
Table tennis

Squash
Golf (match play)
Basketball

Assignment 6

Methods of scoring

The methods of scoring vary widely from one sport to another. In archery under FITA rules (Fédération Internationale de Tiral Arc) at Olympic level, for example, competitors shoot two rounds, comprising a total of 288 arrows from four different distances. Men shoot from a distance of 90m, 70m, 60m, 50m and 30m.

A circular target of 122cm diameter is used at 90m, 70m and 60m distances whilst a circular target of 80cm diameter is used at 50m and 30m. The targets are divided into 10 concentric scoring zones of equal width. They are also divided into five concentric colour zones. The zones give the following scores.

Outer		Inner	
White	1	White	2
Black	3	Black	4
Blue	5	Blue	6
Red	7	Red	8
Gold	9	Gold	10

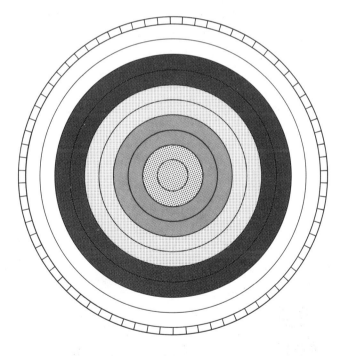

☐	white
■	black
▨	blue
▨	red
▨	gold

Find out how one or more of the following sporting events are scored. Get as much information as possible so that you can describe the full scoring system to a group of beginners in each sport.

Gymnastics	Wrestling
Cricket	Bowls
American football	Windsurfing
Board sailing	Table tennis
Alpine skiing	Skating (freestyle)

 # Assignment 7

Officials in a number of sports are also responsible for ensuring that competitors wear the appropriate clothing and footwear. The umpires in cricket, for instance, must see that the players comply with the following.

> Players must wear white or cream shirts and trousers, with a sweater if necessary. They can also wear a peaked cap or protective helmet. Batsmen and wicketkeepers should wear white pads to guard the lower leg and gloves to protect their hands. Cricket boots may be spiked or have rubber soles.

The clothing and footwear requirements of a
number of sports are given below. Try to work out
to which sports they refer.

Normal dress is worn but competitors must wear target numbers on their backs.

Competitors must wear a number (back and front) as shown in the programme. Clothing must be clean non-transparent, even when wet, and worn so as not to cause offence.

Competitors must wear a racing jersey that covers the shoulders and black shorts reaching approximately to mid thigh. National and international champions and race leaders in stage races may be permitted to wear special jerseys indicating their status.

Players must not wear white clothing but white edging, subject to detailed regulations for major events, is permitted. Match clothes generally consist of a dark shirt and trousers (or shorts) of uniform colour, and flat-soled shoes.

Players wear uniform shorts and jerseys or shirts. Soft leather helmets may be worn to protect the head and ears, but shoulder harnesses and other body armour are forbidden. Studs on a player's boots may be of leather, rubber, aluminium or of an approved plastic, and must conform to specific measurements. Players are not allowed to wear boots with a single stud at the toe.

 ## Assignment 8

Sporting officials are often responsible for ensuring
that only the officially accepted equipment is used.
For example, women javelin throwers must use the
javelins provided at an athletics meeting. They are
not permitted to bring their own models.

Find out as much as you can about the rules
concerning equipment in one or more of the
following sports.

Horse racing	Pole vault
Sailing	Hurdling
Golf	Fencing
Bowls	Croquet
Cycling (Tour de France)	

Assignment 9

Each sport develops its own terminology and the official needs to be familiar with all of them.

State which sport uses each of the following terms and discover the meaning of each of them.

Dump shot	Shooting tab
Boast	Madison Races
Unplayable ball	A left forward pocket
Centre bounce	Scrimmage
The assault	Compulsory exercise
A snapper	Buttresses

 Assignment 10

Select your favourite sporting event and suggest a change in the rules which would have the effect of making the sport either:

(a) more exciting
(b) higher scoring
(c) safer
(d) more suitable for both sexes
or
(e) a combination of two or more of the above.

The economics of sport

AIMS

To gain knowledge and understanding of:

- the level of sports participation in the UK
- the impact of sport on the local economy
- the impact of sport on the national economy

To develop the skills of:

- obtaining information from a variety of sources
- analysis and interpretation of information
- role play

Sport can be exciting, frustrating and morale boosting. It can also absorb leisure time and present employment opportunities. As leisure time has increased and the general standard of living has risen in many developed countries, so the sports business has become a major industry.

In 1985 the Sports Council commissioned the Henley Centre for Forecasting to analyse the impact of sport in the wider economy. Their analysis, *The Economic Impact and Importance of Sport*, was published in 1986 and gives new insights into the increasing economic role of sport in the UK.

Mintel, leading market research publishers in the UK, produced a special report 'The British Sportsman 1986'. The publication was primarily designed for those involved in marketing sports equipment, clothes and footwear sold through high-street outlets. Their research covered levels of sports participation, attitudes to price, the influence of health and the factors which are primarily responsible for taking up sport in the first place.

We will look at some of the findings of these two reports which relate to the sports industry at a national level. There will then be the opportunity to assess the economic impact of sport at a local level.

The individual

Mintel estimate that the average male in full-time employment has 33.5 hours of leisure time each week. The average female has 25.6 hours of leisure time each week. How much of this time is spent in

sport-related activities is open to question. The General Household Survey figures paint quite a positive picture:

Participation in sport in an average month*		
	%	Adult UK population (millions)
Males	54	11.5
Females	35	8.0
Total	44	19.5

* These figures include walking   General Household Survey

The Henley Centre for Forecasting looked at participation within different age groups:

Adult participation in sport by age		
	Indoor sport %	Team sport %
16–24	35	26
25–34	25	16
35–44	24	14
45–59	15	10
60+	10	6

Mintel's figures are not so optimistic. They suggest that in any one week only 12% of the adult population claim to have participated in an individual sport for at least one hour, and only 7% claim to have played a team game.

Mintel calculate that over 9 million people belong to at least one of the 115,000 sports clubs in the country which cater for over 40 different sports. The sports range from football, which has 1.5 million members in 45,000 different clubs, to wrestling, with 6,000 members in 110 clubs.

Sports participation absorbs the individual's finances as well as his or her time. Obviously, spending patterns tend to show the level of affluence of particular households.

Annual household expenditure on sports equipment and subscriptions/admission charges to participant sports in UK			
Gross household weekly income £	Equipment £	Subscription/ Admission £	Total £
99 or less	2.08	3.64	5.72
100–149	5.72	10.40	16.12
150–199	13.52	24.44	37.96
200–249	20.28	31.72	52.0
250–299	30.16	40.56	70.72
300+	89.44	76.96	166.40

Mintel based on Family Expenditure Survey

 Assignment 1

In your groups, design and carry out a survey in order to assess the following for your local area:

(a) The average amount of leisure time for adults
(b) The sports participation levels by age
(c) The leisure spending patterns of the different age groups – be sure to obtain separate figures for males and females
(d) The three most popular non-sporting leisure time activities
(e) The number and type of sports clubs and sporting facilities available locally. Try to find out their membership totals as well as their **subscription charges**

Assignment 2

Look at the three women shown in the photos. One is a full-time student studying for a degree in electrical engineering at a polytechnic. The second has a full-time job as a secretary working in the city. She is married to a solicitor and they have no children. The third is married with two children aged three and six months. She has a part-time job in a local dry cleaners. Her husband is a long-distance lorry driver.

Consider each woman in turn. Do you think that they could have as much time to spend on leisure activities as their male counterparts? Try to work out a typical working day for each of the women in order to see how much of their day is taken up with essential activities and how much time is left for relaxation. Is it possible to improve the ratio of leisure/essential work time for the women? See if you can think of practical ways of ensuring that their leisure time is at least as great as their male counterparts. (For example, husband and wife sharing some of the household tasks, hiring **childminders etc.)**

The economy

The Henley Centre for Forecasting argues that the total sport-related consumer spending (at 1985 market prices) is £4.37 billion. The major contributions to this total include:

Type of spending	£ million
Gambling	1160
Clothing and footwear (including repairs)	770
Sports goods	690
Sports participation	530

Sport certainly accounts for a large proportion of the UK leisure expenditure.

Selected categories of UK consumers' expenditure in 1985	
Category	Expenditure in £ million
Motor vehicles	9916
Beer	8347
(Expenditure by foreign tourists)	(6262)
Cigarettes	6115
Electricity	4360
Furniture and floor coverings	4639
Sport, including gambling	**4366**
Bread	4051
Gas	4046
Menswear	3981
Spirits	3861
Wines and ciders	3847
Sport, excluding gambling	**3207**
DIY goods	2616
Newspapers and magazines	2273
Pets	1278
Records	783
Bingo admissions	288
Cinema	125

Sport also creates wealth, as can be seen in the following assessment of **value added**. Value added is the difference between total revenue and the cost of bought-in materials, services and components.

It is a measure of how much a firm or a sport adds to the bought-in raw materials. When compared with a variety of wealth-creating activities sport comes out in good light.

Comparison of value added in sports related activity to other categories of manufacturing output

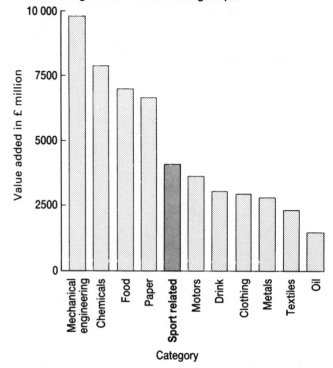

Sport also employs a great number of people:

UK Employment in selected sectors in 1985

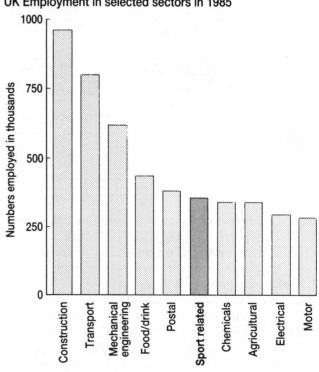

Central and Local Government

A great deal of our sporting facilities are provided by Central or Local Government. We may think that sport is subsidised because it is seen to be of social value. The figures would indicate that the reverse is true – sport adds to the economy rather than feeds from it.

Central Government income from and expenditure on sport (1985)			
Income	**£ million**	**Expenditure**	**£ million**
VAT and excise duties	770	Grants to Sports Councils	37
Betting duty	537	Grants to urban programme	24
Income tax	951	Sport-related component of Rate Support Grant:	
Corporation tax	163	Local authority net expenditure on sport	258
Rail fares	22	Local authority expenditure on education	167
		Central Government employees sports subsidy	27
		Factor expenditure	17
		British Rail: wages etc.	9
		inputs	6
Total income	**2443**	**Total expenditure**	**545**

Central Government also benefits from both direct and indirect tax paid by the voluntary sector of sport. For example, rates paid by a local hockey club for land which clubs own, or VAT paid on bar receipts. Those taxes far outweigh the grants given by central government to voluntary sporting organisations.

Local Government income from and expenditure on sport (1985)			
Income	**£ million**	**Expenditure**	**£ million**
Local authority sports facilities		Direct gross expenditure	
Fees and charges to the public	134	Wages etc.	287
Sales of equipment	24	Running expenses	244
Spectator clubs payment for policing	3	Central departmental administration	90
Other income	13	Education	
Grants from Central Government		Wages etc.	180
To fund net expenditure on sport	258	Other	120
To fund sport and PE education	167	Urban programme	24
To fund capital expenditure	10	Policing for sports events	3
Urban programme	24	Local Government employees sports subsidy	31
Rates	120	Grants to the voluntary sector	2
		Non-monetary expenditure (subsidy to voluntary sector for 'dual use')	9
Total income	**753**	**Total expenditure**	**990**

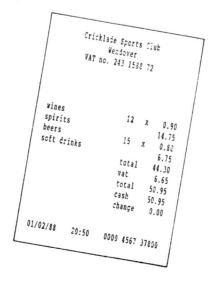

Assignment 3

Conduct a survey in order to assess the impact of sport on the local economy. You will need to investigate the following:

1 The number of people employed locally (if any) in the following sectors:

Commercial sport
spectator clubs
participation clubs
equipment retailers
sportswear retailers
book retailers
equipment manufacturers
sportswear manufacturers
printing and publishing
TV and radio

Voluntary sport
administrators
coaches
referees
bar staff, cleaners etc.

Local Government
staffing connected with leisure/recreation
teaching staff involved with sport

Discuss with your lecturer or teacher how best to obtain all this information. It will be wise to split the group up so that the same information is not sought by a number of different people.

2 The amount the local authority spends on sport and recreation each year. Find out which local councillors are on the recreation committee and invite one of them into your school and/or college in order to get a more accurate picture.

 Assignment 4

The national figures show that sport makes a significant contribution to the economy of this country. Many sporting groups suggest that this should be recognised by the Government and that more money should be used to create better sporting facilities in all parts of the country.

Other pressure groups would argue that sport already has too much money spent on it and that more money ought to be spent on the National Health Service, defence or a number of other vital areas.

Set up a debate within your group. The motion is 'The Government should spend a much larger amount of its money on sport and leisure facilities than it does at the moment.'

You need four people to take on each of the roles given below. You will also need a Chairperson to manage the debate.

Organisation of debate

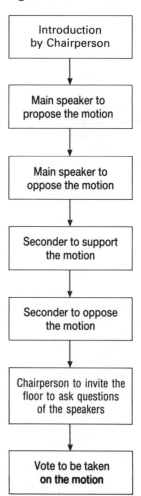

For the motion

Main speaker
Michael Dowgiel – 42 years old with two children of secondary school age. Works for the local authority in the Planning Department. Michael is Chairman of the local Sports Council and a very keen squash player (he has been the local league champion for the last two years).

Michael is angry that his children do not get much opportunity for sport in school and that the local authority provision for sport and leisure is second-rate when compared with other local areas.

Seconder
Wendy Chambers – 18 years old, unemployed since leaving school despite gaining four good CSE passes and a CPVE. Wendy has represented Great Britain as a junior in the 400m hurdles and is currently being sponsored by a local paint manufacturer. She is still finding difficulty in making ends meet and is frustrated that she still has to be supported by her parents. She is waiting to see if her application for a sports scholarship in an American university has been successful.

Against the motion

Main speaker
Councillor Olivia Mutton – 52 years old with three grown-up children. Chairperson of the local council and a keen supporter of free enterprise. She strongly believes that people should pay their way in life and does not support the policy of providing free sporting equipment and facilities to all members of the public. Mrs Mutton considers that if there is a demand for extra sporting facilities then private enterprise will set up the necessary facilities and run them efficiently.

Seconder
Doctor Donald Dakar – 46-year-old consultant surgeon at the local general hospital. Although once an average rugby player, he now believes that sport is responsible for much unnecessary pain and suffering as a result of injury. Would like to see more money being allocated to the National Health Service in order to improve staffing, facilities and equipment.

Sports equipment

AIMS

To gain knowledge and understanding of:

- the employment opportunities in the manufacturing and retailing of sportswear and equipment

- the roles and responsibilities associated with employment in the sports goods manufacturing and retailing industries

- the implications of changing shopping patterns on retailing

- the organisation and administration of a large sports retailing concern

- the role of information technology in the sports retailing industry

To develop the skills of:

- selecting information
- interpreting information
- problem-solving
- numeracy
- interviewing

The manufacture and selling of sports footwear, clothing and equipment is big business. It employs over 83,000 people and contributed £709 million value added to the British economy in 1985. (Reminder: 'value added' is the difference between total revenue and the cost of bought-in materials, services and components. It is a measure of how much a firm adds to the bought-in raw materials.)

There are hundreds of manufacturers (some extremely small) involved in the production of footwear, clothing and equipment whilst over 2,500 specialist shops are involved in the retailing of sports goods.

The largest sports operation in the UK is Dunlop Slazenger International Limited which has an annual turnover (the amount of total sales) in excess of £100 million. This company manufactures tennis balls, tennis, badminton and squash rackets, cricket bats, golf clubs and balls and sports shoes in its various factories in this country. It also imports a lot of footwear, clothing and equipment from abroad. Other large manufacturers and importers include Adidas, Nike UK Ltd, Hi Tec and Reebok UK Ltd.

Sports clothing and equipment is big business.

The small independent high-street sports shops have been hit by many changes over the last few years. They used to be virtually the only retailers of sports clothing and equipment but now these goods can be bought in large supermarket chains, garages, and through mail-order catalogues. This is particularly true of clothing and footwear which yield high profit margins.

A number of specialist retail sports chains and co-operatives have also started to take trade from the sole trader or small partnerships. These chains and co-operatives, using their greater purchasing power, more comprehensive marketing, better staff training and own brand labels, can often display a wider range of goods at more competitive prices than the independent high-street sports shop.

Sports retailers have now started to take note of the popularity of out-of-town stores which have developed over the last few years. Recognising the fact that most households now have a car, DIY and food companies such as Tesco, Sainsbury's and Texas have built huge shops with ample car-parking space outside the very expensive and therefore highly restrictive town centres. All these stores are sited so that they have a very large catchment of potential customers within 10–15 minutes' car travel of the store.

One sports chain which followed this trend is Astral Sports Superstores. Let us look at one of their superstores in detail.

ASTRAL
SPORTS SUPERSTORES
wholly owned subsidiary of House of Fraser

Location
Geron Way, Edgeware Rd., Staples Corner,
(near Brent Cross) London NW2.

Site
A purpose built store with car parking for 150 cars.

Size
28,000 sq. ft.   sales area 16,000 sq. ft.

Opening Times
Mon., Tues., Wed., Fri. : 10am – 8pm
Thursday   10am – 6pm
Saturday   9am – 5pm

Staffing
50 staff – 25 part-time (minimum 15 hours)

Special Features

- 150 metre running track – all weather surface – centre piece of store
- 'Try before you buy' bowls service
- Ski simulator – twin ski deck with variable slope and providing speeds equivalent of up to 70mph on snow. Ski school available with resident ski instructor.
- Tennis practice area with automatic ball feed
- Golf driving net – with computer stroke-analyser
- Snooker hall with full-size snooker table
- Darts board
- Exercise machines – bikes, weights, rowing machines, etc.

- Potential customers are not only encouraged to use the equipment in order to try out clubs, rackets, cues etc., but it is also possible to have professional coaching in a number of sports.
- Special events are held on a regular basis e.g. ski lessons, golf lessons and keep fit.
- 18 TV screens around the store. They can either show a video appropriate to the particular sports section e.g. cricket coaching in the cricket clothing and equipment section, or all 18 screens can be programmed to show the same video.

Reasons for its success

Staffing

Below the top management are a number of department supervisors who are all experienced in sports retail as well as being specialists in the particular sports for which they are responsible. All other assistants, full- and part-time, are employed because of their practical interest in, and knowledge of, sport. Work rotas are organised so that staff can take part in competitions within their particular sport. Staff training is given by a mixture of in-house training as well as specific information and advice given by manufacturing representatives.

Stock control

Computerised stock control is achieved by electronic point of sale (EPOS) at the tills. Goods are bought directly from manufacturers (no wholesaler being involved), and stock is ordered automatically by the computerised EPOS system.

Market research and marketing

A great deal of market research went into selecting the site. It was chosen with a number of factors in mind, not least of which was the necessity to have a population of at least one million within 30 minutes of the superstore. To ensure that the target population is fully aware of the store, a considerable proportion of the initial investment in the project was put aside for advertising (radio/poster/local press/direct mail), public relations and local sponsorship.

The future

There are plans to establish 20–30 similar superstores across the country. At the moment there are two in London with the third planned for opening by 1988. The intention is that Astral Sports Superstores should become as well known as the DIY and grocery superstores such as Sainsbury's and Tesco.

The results so far

Early indications are that the stores are doing very well. They have exceeded their forecast sales of clothing and equipment by a very healthy margin. This is perhaps related to the 'try before you buy' philosophy which the store employs. It certainly appears that customers find it easier to choose the equipment that actually suits them and so appear more likely to make purchases. The extremely wide range of clothing and footwear as well as equipment allows a customer to kit him or herself out completely for a wide range of sports.

Future developments include an equestrian section which will stock tack as well as outdoor wear. It will also be possible to get a wide variety of sporting equipment repaired and serviced.

 Assignment 1

You are a partner in a very successful sports shop in a town in the south of England with a population of 152,000 within a five-mile radius. You are considering expanding with the intention of setting up a chain of stores over the next few years. You have a potential backer who needs to be persuaded that your plans for expansion are likely to be successful.

You have commissioned a study by ISM (International Sports Marketing) in order to determine which of four possible areas should be selected by you for your next shop. One of the potential sites is an existing sports shop, being sold off because of the current owner's apparent ill health.

ISM has given a brief assessment of this shop's current viability.

Part of the ISM study is shown on the next couple of pages. Make use of their findings to determine the following:

(a) The site to be chosen for your new sports shop. This should include:
   (i) population number
   (ii) type of population
   (iii) proximity to main shopping centre
(b) The type of shop you will develop. This should include details of the following:
   (i) product range
   (ii) marketing, including advertising and special promotions
   (iii) layout of shop and window displays
   (iv) staffing and staff training
   (v) stock control
   (vi) future development
   (vii) use of information technology for sales and stock

Present the reasons for your choice in a report to your potential financial backer.

ISM Report on Potential Site for Sports Shop Development

A Southwhich

A sub-regional employment and shopping centre, holiday resort and retirement area on the south coast. Large numbers of commuters to London.

Population	172,000
Communication	Excellent road/rail links to London and SE
Schools/ colleges	A mixture of old schools and new purpose-built comprehensives with excellent sporting facilities. Fall in school age population has led to a number of 'half-empty' schools
Sports club/ facilities	Large number of well-established sports clubs. Water sports particularly well catered for
Site	New shopping precinct within the town centre. Premises of varying sizes possible
Competition	One water-sports specialist. Two general sports shops

B Burkenstead Newtown

Employment centre for immediate area as well as wide part of north Berkshire. It has attracted a large number of new technology industries.

Population	182,000
Communication	Excellent – new motorway link to M25
Schools/ colleges	Number of relatively new and well-built schools – number of sports halls provided
Sports club/ facilities	Excellent range of indoor and outdoor public sports facilities and numerous clubs
Site	Small shop (600 sq. ft available in new regional shopping precinct which attracts customers from whole of Berkshire)
Competition	New sports superstore established on the edge of town. Has not yet built up a strong following

C Eastead

Large urban conurbation seven miles from central London

Population	100,000 but 1.25 million within 15-minute car ride
Communication	Traffic black spot at present. Road improvements taking place
Schools/ colleges	60 infant, 12 comprehensive, two colleges of FE
Sports clubs/ facilities	Large number of sports clubs, very strong athletics club, very strong basketball area
Site	On new shopping development area – four large superstores already on site
Competition	Large number of small independent high-street shops within five-mile radius – well supported by clubs

D Nantcombe

The main commercial centre for NW Berkshire and an industrial centre for a wide area. University and garrison town.

Population	127,000+
Communication	Good communications system – both road and rail
Schools/ colleges	18 primary and three comprehensive schools and University of Berkshire. Good, but old, sports facilities
Sports clubs/ facilities	One sports centre and university facilities. Numerous sports clubs
Site	Existing sports shop (Pentangle) situated in an older part of the town. A number of nearby retail premises have been vacated
Competition	One general sports shop (Olympic Sports) which caters mainly for university students

ISM Extract from Report on Pentangle Sports

Site

Development of shopping centre on the north side of the town has drawn custom away from the high-street area. The position has been made worse by the recent vacation of two adjacent shops by Woolworths and Boots.

The rent and rates of the premises are low and this has helped to keep overheads down.

Market survey

There is a great deal of sport taking place in Nantcombe. Although the University and garrison facilities are mainly used by their own personnel, there are still ample facilities, both indoor and out for the rest of the sporting population.

Our survey revealed the following:

A Schools and the University obtain the bulk of their sporting clothing and equipment from Berkshire County Supplies.

B Sports clothing, footwear and equipment was obtained in the following way by the people surveyed (200):

Sports purchase survey: places where 200 residents bought sports goods

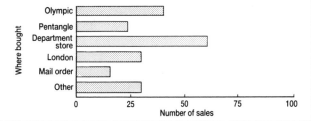

C   The 5 most popular sports were as follows:

    Swimming
    Soccer
    Keep fit/aerobics
    Cricket
    Athletics

    Sixteen different sports were mentioned by respondents in the survey including shooting, show jumping and trampoline.

D   74% know the name and location of the Olympic Sports Shop. 42% knew the name and location of the Pentangle Sports Shop.

Product range

The results above were not reflected in the stock being held by Pentangle. A large proportion of both space and capital was tied up with shooting equipment (guns and ammunition) despite the fact that this sport accounted for only 10% of sales over the previous year.

It was clear that much of the stock, particularly clothing had been on display for some period of time. Over-ordering during the football season had led to a good deal of soccer and rugby clothing which was taking up space and preventing more relevant sporting lines from being displayed. There is a real need to base future orders on actual sales rather than on pure optimism. It was also noticeable that most of the clothing/footwear was not well-known brand names.

Advertising

The manager was well-known locally for his shooting prowess (National Smallbore Champion 1976–8) but he had not used his fame to good effect. He had made no efforts to contact local sporting clubs about club kit discounts, special orders etc. and he had not advertised his shop in the local papers for at least three years. 'There's no need, everyone knows we're here' he said.

Staffing

The manager has two assistants. Both are at present internationals in the shooting world. Both work on a part-time basis, helping out when the manager is involved in competitions.

Summary

Although not a prime site, it is clear that Pentangle could become a profitable concern if appropriate steps are taken. These would include the following:

1   Decide on type of market.
2   Go for brand leaders because customers are aware of their image and believe them to be creditable.
3   A thorough stocktaking exercise should be carried out immediately. Once this is completed then a much more efficient system will have to be developed in order to know accurately and quickly what you have in stock.
4   The shop frontage needs to be brightened up and made more eye catching. The window display needs to be made more exciting and changed more regularly.
5   The present system of stock display is untidy and confusing. Invest in modern fitted display systems that will show your stock to good effect. Make separate display areas for each sporting area. Stock must be kept moving.
6   You need to put in an enthusiastic and experienced manager to make the shop take off.

Assignment 2

Imagine you are the new manager of Pentangle Sports. Use the information given in the earlier part of the ISM report on Pentangle Sports in order to fill in the immediate priorities you would need to undertake. Remember you want the shop to be a success.

Priorities

(a) Market the shop within the locality – advertise in the local newspapers and on local radio.
(b) ?
(c) ?
(d) ?
(e) ?

Assignment 3

You have just been appointed as an assistant in the Pentangle Sports Shop in Nantcombe. The shop is in a mess and the new manager has asked you to sort out the stock so that it can be displayed more attractively.

Choose the correct name for the following pieces of sporting equipment and place them against the appropriate sport.

judogi
brassie
back board
pitons
bob fly
hoop
karabiner
bracer
kicking strap
puck
stabilisers
foil

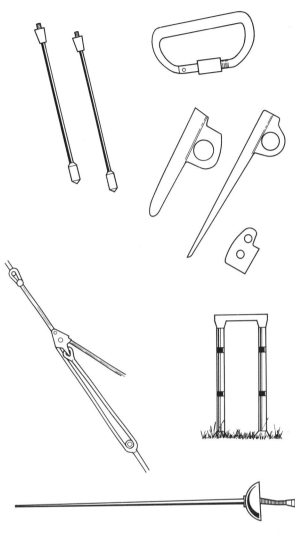

Sport	Equipment
Fishing	
Golf	
Martial art	
Climbing	
Fencing	
Sailing	
Basketball	
Croquet	
Ice hockey	
Archery	

Assignment 4

The manager has decided to have a clear-out sale before restocking the shop. Shoes are to be sold at 15% discount, clothing at 20% and sporting equipment at 12.5% discount.

Calculate the sale prices of the following and work out the total revenue if all the goods are sold.

Item	Amount	Cost
Reebok trainers	3 dozen pairs	£25.00 pair
Adiko hockey boots	1 dozen pairs	£20.00 pair
Springbok running shoes	9 pairs	£32.00 pair
Ladies' leotards (medium)	10	£9.50
Poza sweat top (large)	8	£19.99
Boys' football shirts (asstd)	4 dozen	£6.00
Sabido golf clubs	2 sets	£300.00 set
Sabido golf balls (practice)	4 dozen	£5.00 dozen
Trampoline	1	£800.00

Assignment 5

Trainee Management
& Sales Staff
at

PARRODS

Exciting vacancies for full-time
sales people in our new

SPORTS DEPARTMENT

at our London store.
Must have outgoing attractive personality
and sound practical knowledge and ability
in one or more sporting events.
Full training given.
For an appointment ring Personnel
on **216 97654**

In response to the above advertisement in one of the London evening papers, a large number of people applied for posts within Parrods Sports Department. The best four applicants are to be interviewed. There are three posts available but appointments should be made only if the candidates are suitable.

Members of your class/group should take on one of the following roles:

Interview panel: Sports Department Manager
(Chairperson of panel): Peter Fry
Personnel Manager: June Allott
Marketing Director: Aktar Saleem
Candidates: Gladwyn Twyford
Sheila Babdon
Russell Ayres
Tessa Kwasny
Observers: the remainder of the class/group

Interview arrangement

10–15 minutes. Interview panel to decide upon questions, room layout etc.

Interviews

10 minutes for each candidate.
Decision-making and notifying candidates: 10–15 minutes.

Brief profiles of interviewing panel

Peter Fry, Manager – Parrods Sports Department
42 years old, former professional footballer who invested some of his money into two small sports shops 15 years ago. Shops did not do well and eventually he sold out in order to reduce his losses. Was appointed as manager of the Sports Department of the Swildon branch of Marps and Spenders four years ago and the department has gone from strength to strength. Appointed to this present post two months ago. Keen to get some hardworking and knowledgeable staff to join him.

June Allott, Personnel Manager, Parrods
32 years old, a very keen tennis player who has been with the store for three years. Was on the interviewing panel which appointed Peter Fry, but did not actually want him to be appointed. Thought that he was rather limited in his sporting knowledge, there being many areas of sport of which he appeared to have only a hazy grasp.

Aktar Saleem, Marketing Director, Parrods
52 years old, very keen football supporter with a rather limited knowledge of most other sports. Been with Parrods for 18 years and only appoints people who he believes will be loyal to the store.

The Candidates

Gladwyn Twyford
18 years old, just completed two-year YTS Course at a local printers. Left school with three GCSEs (English, Maths and Physical Education). Very good sportsman. Has represented his county at athletics (high hurdles) and rugby whilst at school and is a loyal team member of Rockton Athletic Club.

Sheila Babdon
17 years old, just completed a CPVE Course with preparatory modules in Retailing, Business Administration and Sports Management. Spends most of her spare time training or competing at trampolining. She is currently ranked third in the country for her age group.

Tessa Kwasny
19 years old, left school at 16 with no qualifications but with a mass of medals and certificates for judo. She is the current national champion for her weight and age group and spends all of her time training and competing. Now feels that she ought to think about a career which she can continue once she finishes with her judo.

Russell Ayres
17 years old, gained seven good GCSE passes and is about to take 'A' levels in English and Business Studies. Short-sighted and not a very able sportsman, but a very keen and knowledgeable sports fan. Recently won the Sports Mastermind Competition on local radio. Works in Kesto's, a large supermarket, on two evenings a week and all day Saturday.

The Observers

It is your task to observe and make brief notes on how both the candidates and the interviewers perform. At the end of the session you will be expected to report back to the whole group with your thoughts.

The magic sponge

AIMS

To develop an understanding and knowledge of:

- the risk of injury when taking part in sporting activities and the wisdom of adequately insuring against such risk

- the comparative risk of injury in a wide variety of sports

- knowledge of insurance as applied to sporting activities

To develop the skills of:

- selecting information

- interpreting visual information

- form completion

- basic numeracy

Assignment 1

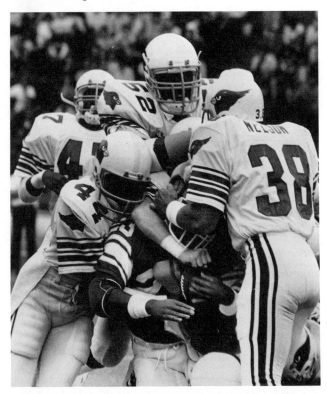

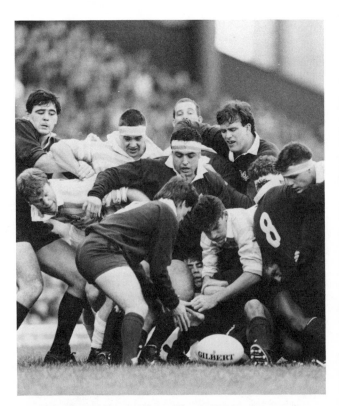

The Saturn Alliance Insurance plc is a well-established insurance company which has specialised in personal accident insurance for the last 30 years. Two years ago the directors of the company set up a sister company to deal with all kinds of sports insurance. The new company, the Magic Sponge Sports Club Insurance plc, quickly cornered a niche in the market and the directors have decided to widen the range of sporting clubs which they cover.

You have just joined the office staff at the Magic
Sponge plc and find that staff shortages have
resulted in a great number of tasks being placed on
your desk. You are keen to do well and set to work
immediately. You receive the following memo:

MEMORANDUM

From: John Drake   To: Date: 30 November 1987

Sorry to drop this on you in your first week, but we need some really
quick decisions. As you can see from our publicity leaflet and
proposal forms, there is a wide gap between what we say we will insure
and what we actually include in our sports charts.

Please extend the number of quoted sports and use your undoubted knowledge
of sporting injuries to put each sport into the most appropriate
insurance category. You are free to add any ones that I may have missed
out.

Return completed by Friday.

John Drake.

Magic Sponge Sports Insurance

Sports people – you cannot always rely on luck or the
magic sponge to get you up and running again after
injury. When a serious injury strikes, you need the
protection of a specialist sports insurance policy.

Sporting injuries can hurt your pocket as well as your
body. Temporary disablement can stop you working.
Permanent disability can end or severely restrict your
working life. Death can be financially and emotionally
disastrous for your dependents.

Whatever your age, your skill level, or your particular
sport, The Magic Sponge Sports Insurance plc has a
policy for you.

Read on for more details!

What will the insurance policy cover?

You will be covered while

- playing or officiating for your club at home or away
  fixtures

- playing at your club's premises

- taking part in training organised by your club

- taking part in any social event organised by the club

- travelling directly to or directly back from the club's
  away fixtures as part of an organised party under the
  direction of the club

What happens in the case of injury?

You will receive cash help in the form of either a lump sum benefit or income benefit or both.

A lump sum is payable in the event of injury causing death or permanent injury and total loss of sight of one or more eyes or loss of use of one or more limbs or inability to carry on gainful employment.

Income benefit is an amount payable at intervals to suit the member for up to 2 years.

How much will it cost me?

The cost will vary according to the type of sport you play, the number of teams you run or in the case of individual sports the number of playing members you have in your club. It will also vary according to how many units of cover you require.

First, decide which group your sport is in.

Individual sports		Team sports*	
Sport	Group	Sport	Group
Angling	C	Association Football	B
Athletics	C	Cricket	C
Bowls	D	Hockey	B
Caving	A	Netball	D
Cycling	B	Rugby Union	A
Darts	D		
Judo	A		
Snooker	D		
Squash	B		
Swimming	C		

*For the purposes of our policy a team sport is a sport in which it is necessary to have more than one player on one side.

The team policy is calculated by the numbers of teams you run. Individual sports members can only be insured in groups of twenty.

Once you have determined which insurance group your sport is in, use the chart below to work out the premium. Use the appropriate group column and work down according to how many units of cover you require. The more units you choose the more expensive your premium. The amount paid to you in the case of injury will be correspondingly higher.

Team Sports

The premiums are based on the assumption that each team plays on average one game per week. You must inform us if this is not the case as premiums will be lowered or raised accordingly.

Clubs who field more than 5 teams each week are eligible for 10% discount on their total premiums paid.

The minimum policy premium is £30.00.

Individual Sports

The premiums shown below will be charged for every 20 members.

Clubs with more than 100 members will be eligible for 10% discount on their total premiums paid.

The minimum policy premium is £30.00.

Premium per team per year						
Amount payable per year				Number of units	Amount of lump sum	Amount of weekly income
£					£	£
A	B	C	D			
110	75	25	15	1	3,000	6
200	100	40	27	2	6,000	12
250	130	49	35	3	9,000	18
310	150	58	40	4	12,000	24
370	170	64	46	5	15,000	30
425	190	70	51	6	18,000	36
490	215	74	58	7	21,000	42
550	250	78	62	8	24,000	48
590	290	82	65	9	27,000	54
650	530	90	66	10	30,000	60
1180	530	130	80	20	60,000	120

Example: A cricket club with two teams which play one game each week and who decide upon 5 units of cover would pay a premium of £64 per team per year. A player who is injured and makes a claim would be entitled to a lump sum of £15,000 for either death or permanent disability, or £30.00 per week for temporary total disability.

Place the following sports in their appropriate
insurance groupings.

Racket sports
Table tennis
Badminton
Tennis
Squash

Team sports
Football
Volleyball
Basketball
Handball
Rugby
Hockey
Baseball
Korfball
Krachtball
Kaatsen
Waterpolo
Ice hockey

Bowl sports
Billiards
Golf
Bowling
Pétanque

Athletics
Sprint
Middle distance
Long distance
Jump
Throw

Body-orientated sports
Gymnastics
Dancing, ballet
Yoga
Weightlifting
Body building

Displacement without help
Walking
Swimming
Jogging
Orienteering
Climbing
Obstacle race
Speleology
Diving
Skin diving

Displacement with help
Roller skating
Horseback riding
Touristic cycling
Competitive cycling
Parachuting
Gliding
Ice skating
Skiing – Alpine
Skiing – Scandinavian

Waterskiing
Rowing
Canoeing/Kayaking
Sailing
Windsurfing
Motor racing
Car racing
Motor boat

Survival sports
Fishing
Shooting
Hunting
Archery
Fencing
Wrestling
Aikido
Ju-jitsu
Karate
Judo
Boxing

Any other sport you can think of

Assignment 2

☎ **TELEPHONE MESSAGE**   Date: 10·6·87   Time: 10·30 am

A Ms. Collins wanted to speak to you. She is General
Secretary of the Havant Tennis Bowls and Cricket Club. The
club has decided to organise insurance cover, and they have
been recommended to try us for a quote. She left the
following details:

TENNIS – 50 players   6 teams   1 game a week
BOWLS – 70 players   8 teams   2 games a week
CRICKET – 30 players   2 teams   1 game a week

Old Jack Roberts (79 years of age) is in bad health. He
suffered a heart attack whilst celebrating a Bowls Club victory.

Two tennis players killed in car accident 2 years ago whilst
returning from a club match.

Joan

You have received this telephone message.

1 Complete a proposal form (as on p. 62) as far as
   you can for Ms Collins.
2 Decide what other information (if any) you need
   from her before you are able to give her a quote.

Magic Sponge Sports Insurance
SPORTS CLUB PROPOSAL FORM

Name and address of club _____

_____

_____

_____ Postcode _____ Tel. No. _____

Name and address of official to whom all communications are to be addressed:

Name_____

Address_____

_____

_____ Postcode _____ Tel. No. _____

Number of teams:

Number of playing members:

Maximum number of games played each week (ex. tours and festivals): _____

Period of Insurance From [   ] am/pm on [Day | Month | Year] to [Day | Month | Year] ending at midnight

State number of units of cover required (up to maximum of 20):

Each unit provides:
Temporary total disability £6.00 per week
Permanent disability £3,000
Temporary total disability £3,000

Has the club had any previous insurance? If so, when and
with which company?

Has any company or insurer in respect of any of the risks
to which this proposal applies:
a) declined to insure the club?

b) required special terms to insure the club?

c) cancelled or refused to renew the club's insurance?

d) increased the club's premium on renewal?

Details of all accidents to members arising out of any club sport or assignment occurring during the past 3 years.

Date	Cause of injuries	Nature of injuries	Period of total disablement

Declaration
Very important

You are reminded of the need to disclose any facts which the insurer would take into account in the assessment and acceptance of this proposal. Failure to disclose all relevant facts may invalidate your policy or may result in your policy not operating fully. We declare that the statements and particulars above are to the best of our knowledge and belief true and complete and that this proposal shall form the basis of the contract between us and the Magic Sponge Sport Insurance Plc.

Date   **Signature**

Assignment 3

The managing director has received a letter from the Rugby Football Union complaining that the 2,200 rugby clubs in the country with a total of 44,000 players are having to pay higher premiums than any other amateur sport in the country. They have asked him to justify this state of affairs. The managing director requires you to give him your views on this matter in writing by tomorrow morning.

I ALWAYS THOUGHT BOWLS WAS SUCH A SAFE GAME!

 ## Assignment 4

Your new extended list of sports groupings which the Magic Sponge Sports Insurance plc has accepted and marketed has resulted in a massive increase in business. The office staff are overwhelmed and you have been asked to calculate the premiums for the following proposals.

(a) Sea Angling Club – 12 members – all fit – they want to receive maximum cover.
(b) The South Wales Speleological Club – 30 members – all fit, no other company has accepted them so far. They want maximum cover.
(c) Barking District Football Association – a district application involving 40 teams/500 players. They want 6 units of cover.

 ## Assignment 5

Your company has had to settle a number of recent claims for sporting injuries which could have been avoided if the claimants had behaved more sensibly.

Draw up a set of safety guidelines which could be sent out with proposal forms. The guidelines should help both individual and team sports members to avoid unnecessary accidents. Be sure to include all possible areas of potential danger.

 ## Assignment 6

A number of requests have been received asking for advice on what to include in a first-aid kit. The kit should be small enough to take to away games but comprehensive enough to cope with most normal mishaps. Produce an information sheet to satisfy these requests. If you consider that some sports have particular requirements then please be sure to include these in your information sheets.

Sporting origins

AIMS

To gain knowledge and understanding of:

- the sports that people play
- the variety of sporting activities which take place throughout the world
- the influence of the media on sporting interests
- a number of individual sports

To develop the skills of:

- secondary research – historical and cultural
- written communication
- analysis

At Eton School an annual contest takes place which is known as the 'Eton Wall Game'. It is unique to the school and its origins are obscure. Outside of the school there is no interest in the activity as a sport.

It is played by two sides of ten players on a narrow strip of ground roughly 118 yards long and four to five yards wide, bounded by an 11-foot high wall along its length. For the spectator it is mainly static with only rare moments of rapid movement, as each team tries to force their players and the ball through the opposition to the goal.

The American Football Superbowl Final is played in front of a crowd of 100,000. Television carries the sport to millions of people in scores of countries throughout the world. The only place where this all-American game is played professionally is in the USA.

Cricket originated and developed in England. It was exported to the British Empire where, although most countries have broken their links with the Empire, it has remained extremely popular. Outside these countries (such as Australia, West Indies, India, Pakistan) it is almost totally ignored, although Papua New Guinea has adapted it to its own needs as a substitute game for war!

The distribution of sports around the world is a complex phenomenon, with many and varied reasons for some sports remaining purely local and others becoming truly international.

Distribution may be related to the nature of the rules of play, the type of equipment or facilities required, the qualities demanded of competitors and the traditions and history of a country.

 ## Assignment 1

Bear in mind the above points about the distribution of sports, and in groups discuss and try to explain the following situations. You might find a sports encyclopaedia from your library helpful, for example *The Oxford Companion to Sports and Games* edited by John Arlott.

1   Tossing the caber is largely unknown outside Scotland and the north of England.

2   Boule is extremely popular in France but virtually non-existent in England.

3   Many different forms of unarmed combat originated in Japan.

4   Hurling is an exclusively Irish game.

5   Finland always produces outstanding javelin throwers and long-distance runners.

6   For such a small country, Sweden produces very many top-ranked tennis players.

7   American football is only played professionally in the USA.

8   Although wrestling is an Olympic sport, Cumberland wrestling remains of local interest only.

9   The Australians have developed their own particular form of football known as Australian Rules Football.

Can you add any more interesting examples of countries and their sports to this list?

Choose one continent from America, Africa, Asia and Europe and draw an outline map, naming the major countries. Add the major sports for the countries named. See if you can find any patterns in the distribution of sports.

 ## Assignment 2

Distribution of sports

Distribution of sports			
Local (sport played only in one region of a country)	One country	Many countries	International (throughout the world)
Cumberland wrestling Tossing the caber in Scotland	Boule in France Pelota in Spain Hurling in Ireland Sumo wrestling in Japan Real tennis in Britain	Cricket } Commonwealth Bowls } Martial arts } Far East Basketball } Baseball } Under US influence American football }	Soccer Athletics Tennis Boxing Golf

These are not watertight compartments. Try to:

(i) add other sports to the categories
(ii) **explain why some sports do not fit neatly anywhere**

For example, rugby union is played throughout Britain, but rugby league is played only in the north. Both codes are played in some commonwealth countries but not in all; however, **they are both played in France but not in any other European countries at the highest level.**

Assignment 3

An implanted sport

Before the start of Channel 4 television in 1982, little was known about American football in Britain. It was regarded as some gigantic game of chess played by padded giants in short bursts of unbelievable physical violence. For most people brought up on a diet of fair play and sport for its own sake it was a non-starter. The media paid it no attention and grave doubts were expressed about the wisdom of Channel 4 wasting so much effort in trying to establish it.

Today, interest in the sport is high, clubs and leagues have been formed, many of the teams and players in the USA are almost household names in Britain and regular reports, feature articles and photos appear in the newspapers. This has largely been as a result of television exposure.

Write a letter to your local Sports Council explaining why you think American football or any other sport you would like to play should be promoted in your locality.

Explain how you think the sport could be developed and what should be provided in terms of facilities, equipment, coaches and courses.

 Assignment 4

Related sports

Copy out and complete this table. You may need to do some research. Perhaps you can add some other variations on football.

Type of football	Number of players		Type of goals	Method of scoring	Major differences in contact rules
	in squad	on pitch			
Rugby league					
Rugby union					
Soccer					
Gaelic football					
Australian rules football					
American football					

Try to produce similar types of table for other sports with things in common. For example:

racket sports: tennis, squash, badminton, fives, rackets, real tennis.

stick sports: field hockey, roller hockey, shinty, hurling, lacrosse, ice hockey.

ball sports: netball, basketball, handball.

wrestling: Graeco-Roman, freestyle, Cumberland, Sumo.

For each table try to find out which sport was the original form and how others developed from it.

![Assignment 5 logo] **Assignment 5**

Tennis that taxes mind and muscle

A REAL TENNIS court is probably the strangest playing area you will ever see.

Let's start in the middle — the net is strung 5ft high at the posts, but dips to 3ft in the middle. The markings at one end are carefully graded in yards, at the other, only one half is marked as such. To the left of the server are netted galleries running almost the length of the court wall which, if the ball is hit into them, trap it for a fault. Behind the server is a similar netted area called the dedans (a ball returned into it wins the point). Behind the receiver is a small grille — a serve into that wins a point.

From the wall opposite the galleries juts the tambour; any ball hitting it comes off at a usually unplayable angle. Finally, the penthouse is a sloping roof that bounds three sides of the court on which the ball must be served and can be played along it before dropping.

Problems visualising the scene? Well, if I tell you that the game originated in monastery cloisters, perhaps it will become clearer. The galleries and dedans represent the cloister openings, the tambour the buttress of a wall.

The scoring is the same for tennis apart from the chases. Delayed penalty points is the simplest way to describe them, gained when a player fails to return a ball from the hazard area, or when it is hit into one of the non-winning galleries. When two chases are gained, the server and receiver change ends and play the chases which bring into play the marked yard-lines any more explanation and your brain would probably overload — it's simpler when you see a game.

From the *Independent*, January 1987

Because the rules of real tennis are so complicated and the court so peculiar, it is difficult to explain the game simply. No doubt it is much easier to go out and play it!

Choose a sport with which you are familiar and using only 250 words explain how it is played. Imagine you are talking to someone from a different society or culture who has no idea of the activity at all. For example, explain cricket to an American or tennis to an Eskimo. You may add one drawing, diagram or photo to your presentation if you think it will be helpful.

Assignment 6

 Assignment 7

GUESS THE GAME

How many clues do you need?

Clue 1: It is the second fastest team sport in the world, beaten only by ice hockey.

Clue 2: It is a spectacular, but easy-to-play game which is attracting growing interest in Britain.

Clue 3: Played by both men and women, it can take place indoors and out (the pitch is 40m by 20m).

Clue 4: Seven of a twelve-strong squad play at any one time. As in ice hockey, flying substitutions are permitted, except for the goalkeeper.

Clue 5: The ball, similar to a size 3 football, can be passed by any part of the anatomy above the knee.

Clue 6: Players may take three steps with the ball before either bouncing it or passing, while opponents are allowed to block.

Clue 7: Goals are scored by propelling the ball into the net past the keeper from outside the 6m exclusion zone.

Clue 8: The sport, originally from Denmark, is played in 96 countries (with the east Europeans and Scandinavians dominating) and is an accepted Olympic sport.

Give us a clue!

Make a list of games played in Britain which are not very well known to the public, for example, fives, curling or shooting. Use a reference book from a library, or some other accurate source to produce a series of clues which gradually reveal the game. Try to find a photograph or drawing to illustrate the game without making its identity obvious.

These photographs show aspects of different sports played in particular countries of the world. For each example name the sport and one country where it is played.

Now try producing your own sporting links picture quiz.

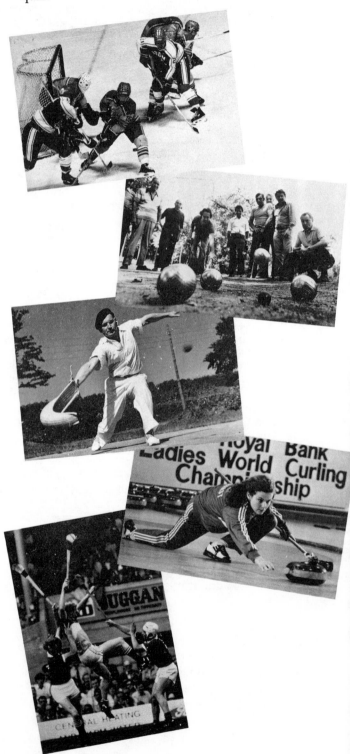

Answer to GUESS THE GAME: handball

Britain's sporting past

AIMS --

To develop an understanding of:

- the development of individual sports and sport in general
- the influence of social history on sports development
- the reasons for change in sport

To develop the skills of:

- secondary research – historical and cultural
- role play
- practical research and experimentation
- interviewing

 Assignment 1

Great moments in sport

1   For each photograph above say
   (a) what had happened?
   (b) who was involved?
   (c) when and where did it take place?

2   Produce your own picture quiz of famous sporting events from the past using photographs and questions.

3 The following list of sporting clues will help you identify a particular year. See how many clues you need before you can correctly guess the year.

> **Clue 1:** T. Seko won the London Marathon.
> **Clue 2:** Lloyd Honeyghan won the world welterweight boxing title.
> **Clue 3:** B. Becker beat I. Lendl in Wimbledon final.
> **Clue 4:** Chicago Bears won the Superbowl.
> **Clue 5:** Liverpool FC completed the double.
> **Clue 6:** Joe Johnson won the world Snooker championship.

4 Compile your own sporting headlines, photographs, event winners for a particular year into a set of clues which you can use to test people's sporting knowledge. Use a variety of sports. Your local library should be able to help you with books and back copies of newspapers and magazines.

 Assignment 2

Reliving the ancient Olympics

Event	Differences from similar modern events
ATHLETICS	
Short sprint (200m)	Use of stone starting blocks with grooves cut in and starting 'gates' at Corinth.
Double sprint (400m)	Two lengths of the stadium using a turning post at the far end of the track.
Long distance	Many stadium lengths using two turning posts. Jostling controlled by umpires!
Long jump	Use of weights called **Halteres** possibly from a standing start.
Discus	Large, flat disc of metal or stone, 6–9 kilos, thrown in the Greek style.
Javelin	Thong wound around the shaft and held in the hand to impart spin to the javelin.
COMBAT SPORTS	No time limits, no weight categories, no ring
Boxing	Leather thongs bound around the hands and wrists instead of gloves.
Wrestling	Matches decided by three falls, that is touching the ground with the knees.
Pankration	Kicking, punching, grappling and throwing until a submission achieved.

Using the table consider the following:

Practical
  (i) Try standing and running long jumps with and without various weights. Compare the results.
 (ii) Experiment with sprint starts using a variety of methods such as blocks, spiked shoes, groove in the ground. Time your sprint over 10 metres and compare your results.
(iii) As a group compare times (and problems caused) by using turning posts in a race.

Theoretical
  (i) Consider the dangers posed by the boxing and pankration events. Compare them with modern sports including judo, Thai boxing and karate.
 (ii) Investigate the similarities and differences between the many types of modern wrestling including freestyle, Graeco-Roman, Cumberland and Westmorland, Sumo, Schwingen, Glima, Sambo, Yagli and Kushti. Draw up a table to compare and contrast the different styles.

Freestyle   Graeco-Roman

Cumberland and Westmorland   Freestyle

Sumo

Assignment 3

Landmarks in the development of football

All sports evolve over a period of time. Change may reflect changes in social conditions, improved technology or different training methods.

Although rugby and association football have remained basically the same this century, a great deal of change took place in earlier times.

From the twelfth century, a form of football had been played between parishes and villages in England and it has survived until the present day.

Football, as played today in its many forms, has its origins in the public schools in the first part of the nineteenth century.

By referring to the chart on p. 72 and researching other sources in libraries, find out:

(i) details of traditional games at Eton, Harrow and Winchester.
(ii) earliest sets of rules for rugby and football.
(iii) why rugby football split into two codes – league and union.
(iv) differences between American football, Gaelic football and Australian rules football.

Choose a sport with which you are not very familiar. Go to reference books in your library and chart the landmarks in the development of the sport. You might like to add photographs and other illustrations to bring the text to life in a form suitable for a wall display.

 ## Assignment 4

Baron Pierre de Coubertin was the inspiration behind the rebirth of the Olympic Games. His dream came true when the first modern Olympic Games were held in the Olympic Stadium in Athens in 1896. However, the games were very modest by comparison with today's extravaganzas. Obviously, since they took place in the days before instant communication it was quite natural that most of the competitors were Greek.

It is said that when one American competitor was asked how he came to be competing, he replied that he had been on holiday at the time in Europe and called in to see what he could enter!

Compare the first of the modern Olympic Games held in Athens in 1896 with the 1984 Los Angeles Games. You will need reference books from the library. The British Olympic Association may be able to help.

(i) Find out how many athletes competed and from which countries they came. (Why will these figures not give a true picture of what should have happened at Los Angeles?)
(ii) Investigate the number of different sports involved, the number of events per sport and whether or not all events are now open to women.
(iii) Find out how the Olympics of 1896 were funded and compare with the methods used in 1984.
(iv) Compare the facilities available on both occasions and the opening ceremonies.
(v) Consider the rewards received by athletes at both games.
(vi) Summarise and explain the reasons for the changes you have noted.

Landmarks in the development of football

1840–60
most boarding and grammar schools adopted football
'One game with many variants'

Dribbling Game	Handling Game
Eton	Rugby
Harrow	Cheltenham
Winchester	Marlborough
Charterhouse	

Difficulties at Oxford and Cambridge Universities for students coming from
a variety of school codes.

1848: First Cambridge rules agreed
1862: Thring's detailed code
1863: Cambridge revised rules

'No hacking, tripping or running with the ball'

ASSOCIATION FOOTBALL

1863: Football Association formed.
1864: FA rules agreed 'no running with ball'.
1872: FA Challenge Cup.
1872: First international match England v Scotland.
1888: Midland Football League founded.
1894: Southern League founded.
1904: Fédération Internationale de Football Associations (F.I.F.A.).
1930: First World Cup.
1966: England win the World Cup.

RUGBY UNION

1870: First international match England v Scotland (20-a-side).
1871: Rugby Football Union.
1875: 15-a-side becomes common.
1888: County championships.
1890: International Rugby Board formed.
1893: RFU voted against broken time payments.
1924: British Lions touring side.
1987: First World Cup.

RUGBY LEAGUE

1895: Northern RFU formed.
1897: Challenge Cup competition.
1906: 13-a-side rule.
1922: Rugby Football league formed.
1948: International Board.

First rules for other football:
American: 1867
Gaelic: 1885
Australian Rules: 1866

The origin of rugby football (with only slight evidence to support the account) at Rugby School:

'This stone commemorates the exploit of William Webb Ellis who, with a fine disregard for the rules of football as played in his time, first took the ball in his arms and ran with it, thus originating the distinctive feature of the **Rugby Game. AD 1823**'.

The Olympic Games: Athens 1896

'The Hero'
Spyros Louis, Greek marathon winner.

'The Athletes' (311)
Australia (1), Austria (4), Chile (1), Bulgaria (1), Denmark (4), France (19), Germany (19), Greece (230), Great Britain (8), Sweden (1), Switzerland (1), Hungary (8) and the USA (14).

Most came on their own initiative and at their own expense.

'The Stadium'

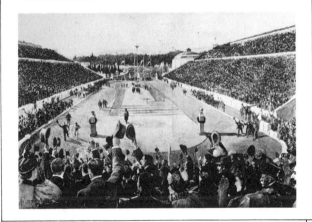

'The Reward'
Only 1st place (silver) and 2nd place (bronze) were recognised.

'The Events'

1	**Athletics**	(12 events): 100m, 400m, 800m, 1500m, marathon, 110m hurdles, high jump, long jump, triple jump, pole vault, shot, discus.
2	**Cycling**	(6 events): 2000m sprint, individual road race, 10,000m track race, 100km track race, 12-hour race, 1,000m time trial.
3	**Fencing**	(2 events): Foil individual, Sabre individual.
4	**Gymnastics**	(8 events): Horizontal bar (individual and team), parallel bar (individual and team), pommel horse, long horse vault, rings, rope climbing.
5	**Shooting**	(5 events): Free pistol, rapid fire pistol, free rifle, military revolver, free rifle – three positions.
6	**Swimming**	(4 events): 100m freestyle, 1200m freestyle, 500m freestyle, 100m freestyle for sailors.
7	**Weightlifting**	(2 events): Heavy weight – one-handed lift and two-handed lift (separately).
8	**Wrestling**	(1 event): Heavy weight.
9	**Tennis**	(2 events): Men's singles, men's doubles.

(Rowing and sailing events were cancelled due to bad weather and cricket was not held because there were no participants! And there were no events for women!)

Assignment 5

Changes in sport

Equipment   Steel to glass fibre poles
in pole vaulting

 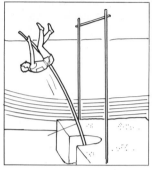

Clothing   Changing fashions in tennis

1980s   1920s

Machines   Technological advances

Rewards   Influence of television on snooker

Winner: £5.00

Rewards: 1987 World
Professional Championship
1st: £80,000
Runner up: £48,000
Total prize fund: £400,000

Footwear   Improved materials and design

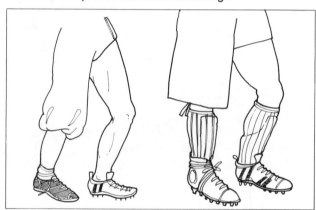

Rules   Formulation of rules and
regulations of boxing

1   Using drawings or photographs, following visits to museums and libraries, illustrate the changes in particular sports by focusing on:

   (a) equipment (e.g. the development of rackets in tennis)
   (b) clothing (e.g. the changes in cricket dress and protection)
   (c) machines (e.g. the improvements in bicycle design and rider equipment)
   (d) rules and regulations (e.g. boxing)

2   Consider how the following have influenced sporting change:

   (a) radio
   (b) television
   (c) newspapers
   (d) books and magazines

Bear in mind such things as popularity, publicity, advertising, rewards, major competitions, public image.

3   Can you think of any sport that has changed very little? Why has it not been affected by change?

4   In pairs, construct a conversation between famous sportsmen and women of past and present in the same sport, for example, W. G. Grace and Ian Botham, or Lottie Dodd and Martina Navratilova talking about the way they play their sport.

Assignment 6

Every picture tells a story

(i) Name the member of the royal family and the likely date of the print.
(ii) Comment on both the dress and equipment used by the players and explain the changes that have since taken place.
(iii) In what ways has the royal family helped to popularise sport in recent years? List the sports and the people involved.

(i) Name the sport and approximate date.
(ii) Explain the changes that have occurred in dress, equipment and technique since then.

(i) Suggest the sport the spectators are following, guess the event and try to fix the period from their dress.
(ii) Consider the ways in which support for sport has changed over the last century.

(i) In what ways would you consider the ladies' dress made playing golf difficult?
(ii) Give an approximate date for the print and explain the social influences on women playing sport at the time.

(Answers at end of chapter)

Make a collection of old sporting photographs with a particular theme, e.g. changing dress. Put them into book form with a written commentary.

Assignment 7

Hall of fame

Lottie Dodd
Wimbledon champion on all five occasions in which she competed between 1887 and 1893. She was only 15 when she first won and was said to have an unfair advantage in being allowed to wear shorter skirts than older women!

Suzanne Lenglen
Wimbledon champion first in 1919, from then only beaten once again in singles in her amateur career. She revolutionised ladies' tennis clothing and dominated the game.

Maureen Connolly
'Little Mo' completed the 'grand slam' of championship wins in 1953, the first by a woman. For the three years up to 1954 she was beaten on only four occasions. A broken leg cut short her career.

Martina Navratilova
Wimbledon champion eight times from 1978. Multi-championship winner whose earnings exceeded £10 million in March 1986. With Chris Lloyd, she is in a different class to other players. Now being challenged by the up-and-coming Steffi Graff.

Every sport has had players who have had a special influence on the activity. It may have been the quality of their play, the introduction of new skills or tactics or a refreshing approach to the game. With some people it has been the nature of their personality, the example set to others or their determination to achieve success.

1   Choose any sport and make a list of all those players who you think made a special contribution to the development of the activity. Reduce your list to a maximum of the 12 most influential.

2   Draw up a checklist to analyse the reasons for their major influence on the game. Use headings such as success, high level of skill, new ideas, changes in play, strong personality, sense of fair play, **determination to succeed, courage and others.**

Assignment 8

Sporting memories

Here are some extracts from an interview with a man who was at school in London from 1914 until 1923:

Yes, we played football every day in the playground, wearing our usual school clothes, big black boots and all. Our caretaker and the school football captain arranged matches against other schools. We played during lunch time in the school playground and the whole school turned out to cheer. Once we were due to play on grass, but when we got there the pitch was not grass but cinders.

I remember a young teacher called Mr Howell who took us for games – football in the winter and cricket in the summer. We only played hockey once and I got a black eye from one of the sticks. Mr Howell also took us for drill in the playground which was lots of exercise and deep breathing, not much fun really.

This woman was at school from 1919 to 1928; here are her memories:

I loved playing netball and was chosen for the school team. We had to wear a navy blue gymslip and a white blouse. The teacher gave me a gymslip as I didn't have one. Miss Smith, the netball teacher, also took us for running games in the playground and athletics. I liked high jump and the relays, especially running in the class team. Another thing I liked was drill in the playground. Our class teacher would take us all out and we would swing our arms and stretch in time with her instructions. The only time I used a vaulting horse was when I left school and joined the Martinsville Ladies' Club.

Arrange to interview a person who was at school before the beginning of the last war (1939).

Draw up a checklist of questions to ask including activities undertaken in school and outside of school, which members of staff were involved, type of clothing worn and equipment used, and facilities available.

Ask permission to tape record your interview. Turn your interview into a report for your local paper entitled 'School sport fifty years ago' or similar.

See appendix (page 113) for guidelines on interviewing techniques.

Answers to sporting prints

Photograph 1: The Prince of Wales playing tennis at Baden-Baden 1883
Photograph 2: A game of cricket played on the Artillery Ground, London in 1743
Photograph 3: Cup Final scenes in London in 1906
Photograph 43: Ladies' Golf Club at Westward Ho! in Devon at the turn of century

Sport as a political football

AIMS

To develop knowledge and understanding of:

- the origins of the modern Olympic Games
- the way politics and sport have been used together
- the way political problems currently impinge on sporting participation

To develop the skills of:

- communication
- historical research
- group activity
- role play
- problem-solving
- decision-making

 Assignment 1

What's going on?

For each newsflash about the Olympic Games, write down the year and city in which the Games were held, together with full details of the incident reported. In your library you will find reference books and sports history books which describe the Olympics. The British Olympic Association also publishes an official report after each Olympic Games.

For a city crippled by the expense of staging the Games, the walk-out of the black African nations and their friends is the last straw.

It is reliably reported that a number of athletes in the Olympic village have been taken hostage by gunmen. Some shooting was heard but a news blackout has been imposed.

A short while ago the Führer left the Stadium. No reason was given for his abrupt departure. Jesse Owens has just won a gold medal in the long jump.

The Soviet team official complained that not only did the blatant commercialism insult the spirit of the Games, but more importantly the safety of his team could not be guaranteed by the host city.

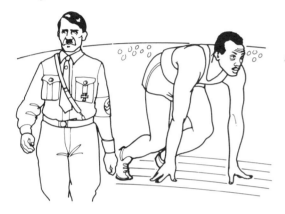

At the medal ceremony the gold and bronze medal winners raised gloved fists above their heads while their national anthem played.

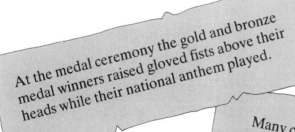

Many countries were missing from the opening parade today. The British representative marched alone carrying the Olympic flag.

Assignment 2

Consider the following imaginary letter from Pierre
de Coubertin, the founder of the modern Olympic
Games, to the current President of the International
Olympic Committee.

Dear Mr. President,

Although my name may remind you of the early days of
our Olympic movement, I am compelled to say that little of what
I said or did seems to have been remembered!

What has caused this great movement to tear itself apart
and fall from the high ideals I set so long ago? Where is the true
spirit of Olympianism? What has happened to the idea of taking
part for its own sake?

How could league tables of medal winners be permitted?
Where are the great festivals of art, music and literature to run
alongside the athletic contests? How can you allow people to
train full time, to be paid, to receive every possible help and then
still to be called amateurs and to compete in our Games?

As for boycotts, walk-outs, demonstrations, squabbles over
flags and nationalities, this movement was intended to help the
cause of peace in the world not to emphasise and encourage
differences between nations.

I remember saying that I restored the Games 'in order
to ennoble and strengthen sports, in order to assure their independence
and duration and thus to set them better to fill the educational
role which devolves upon them in the modern world.'

What has happened to my dream?

Sincerely,
Baron de Coubertin

1 Find out about de Coubertin's background and how he set about recreating the ancient Olympics in modern form. Explain what he meant by an 'educational' role for sport. Write your description in 500 words as an entry in a new publication called the *Who's Who of Sport*.

2 Draft a letter in reply to de Coubertin from the President of the IOC. Explain how and why the Games have changed, what has been achieved by the IOC and what problems remain to be solved.

3 Invite an official from the British Olympic Association to speak to your group to explain how they promote the Olympic Movement.

Problems	Host city	Year
Controversy over award to city		
Nationality/eligibility problem		
Demonstrations prior to event		
Crippling financial cost		
Problems with communication equipment		
Boycotts		
Cheating (drugs, etc.)		
Demonstrations by athletes		
Terrorist attacks		
Bad weather/location problems		

 Assignment 3

Problems, problems!

1 Copy out and complete the following table which lists the problems that have arisen at various Olympic Games since 1956. You will probably need to refer to the library books you used in the first assignment in this module.

2 Use the problems listed above, and any others you would consider relevant, to complete this board game.

Assignment 4

JUAN GARCÍA
PRESIDENT IOC
SEOUL

DENNIS – WAR HAS BROKEN OUT BETWEEN
NORTH AND SOUTH KOREA.

GAMES FACILITIES DESTROYED IN BOMBING RAID
TOTALLY IMPOSSIBLE TO STAGE 1988 OLYMPIC
GAMES HERE.
IOC EMERGENCY COMMITTEE MET TODAY.
BIRMINGHAM PROPOSED AS SUBSTITUTE VENUE IN
VIEW OF OUTSTANDING PROPOSALS FOR 1992 GAMES.
IF ACCEPTABLE BRITISH GOVERNMENT WILL BE
APPROACHED FORMALLY THIS WEEK – JUAN.

DENNIS HOWETTS, M.P.
LONDON

Trevor McGill,   Room 115,
Professor of Political Studies,   House of Commons,
University of Birmingham.   Westminster

Dear Trevor

     Just to confirm what I said on the phone this morning. We have exactly one
week in which to decide whether or not we can stage the Games in Birmingham this
summer. Obviously this is a wonderful opportunity but we must be sure we can
handle everything

     I have no doubt that the actual facilities – both venues and accommodation –
will be up to standard and ready on time. What concerns me are the complex political
issues and I would like your advice on a number of points which I have listed
separately.

     Obviously the strictest confidence will be observed, so do be frank.
I'm expecting a call from the PM at any time, so your early attention to this
would be appreciated.

     To help you make your comments I have asked the British Olympic Association
to send you a copy of the rules of the International Olympic Committee (IOC).
As you know the IOC controls all aspects of the Olympic Games, including the
eligibility of countries and individual competitors and we must be up to date with
any rule changes.

                              Yours sincerely,

                              Dennis
                              Dennis Howetts

MEMORANDUM

To: T McGill   From: D Howetts   Date: 9 July

URGENT AND CONFIDENTIAL

OLYMPIC ISSUES - PLEASE COMMENT AS FULLY AS POSSIBLE

1 Since North and South Korea are currently at war with one another,
is either country allowed to compete in the Olympic Games? Would a
cease-fire in Korea alter their eligibility? What would happen if they
were allowed to take part and their teams or individuals were due to
compete directly against each other?

2 The boycott of the Moscow Olympics in 1980 by USA and its allies was
followed on a tit-for-tat basis by the refusal of the USSR and its friends
to attend the 1984 Los Angeles Games. Can we be sure that both sides will
compete in Birmingham?

3 Although South Africa is still banned from the Olympic Movement, British
sportsmen and sportswomen do compete in South Africa. The Zola Budd
controversy continues and many countries boycotted the 1986 Commonwealth
Games in Edinburgh.
    Is it likely that a British venue will provoke another walk-out by black
African nations?

4 In Los Angeles, competitors from both Taiwan and the People's Republic
of China competed together. How did this come about? Should we assume
that there will be no problems between these two countries, especially
since Hong Kong is such a delicate issue with China at present.

5 Israel is regularly refused entry to the Asian Games on the grounds of
security. In view of the events of 1972 and the continuing turmoil in the
Middle East, should we aim to have Israel excluded? Also do you think it
likely that the IOC will support a move to have the Palestine Liberation
Organisation as a competing nation?

6 There are a number of other worries over individual nations:

   i) Human rights appear to be ignored in Chile. Will some countries
      refuse to compete against Chile?

  ii) Britain and Argentina are still technically at war. Would
      Argentina be prepared to compete against Falkland Island
      representatives?

iii) The USA actively supports opponents of Nicaragua's government. Would the USA take part against a country they openly oppose?

iv) Would the internal problems of Sri Lanka spill over into the Olympics, given the considerable number of Tamil refugees in Britain?

8   In order to reduce nationalistic feelings at the Games, I would suggest that we propose the following alterations to the Games to the IOC at their next meeting.

i) The opening ceremony to be devoid of national flags and uniforms. Teams to march behind their country's name, wearing their own clothing, to reflect their individuality.

ii) At the victory ceremony, medals and flowers will be presented followed by the official Olympic fanfare. There will be no national flags or anthems.

iii) Member countries of the IOC will prevent publication of any tally of medals won by individual countries.

8   Finally, given all these potential difficulties, are the problems too risky, in your opinion, for us to accept the Games? Should I tell the PM to say no?

 Assignment 5

'On the Spot'

Organise your group to play 'On the Spot'. You need a minimum of six people, divided into the following categories:

(a) Question master to ask questions and keep the score.
(b) Audience of at least two people to give marks on a scale of 1–5 for convincing nature of the panel member's answer.
(c) Panel members, at least three, to answer questions within their assigned role.

First, decide which area of sporting politics is to be investigated, then choose characters for the panel. You now need to draw up a list of questions (usually a maximum of 10). It would be helpful for the group to research the topic before playing the game.

Example:

Topic: South Africa and World Sport

Potential panel members (four to be chosen):

Anna Vanhoren: 15, white schoolgirl from Johannesburg, national long-jump champion.

Miriam Tootli: 16, black shopworker from Soweto, good all-round sportswoman.

Indira Singh: 43, Indian factory worker from Port Elizabeth, children all play hockey.

Tomas Burg: 56, white farmer from Transvaal, former rugby international, chairman rugby club.

Derek Kingsbury: 32, coloured teacher from Durban, captain local cricket club.

Steve Mysonga: 21, black ANC member in hiding, formerly from Sharpeville and a junior sprint champion.

Suggested questions (to be asked of each panel member in turn):

1 From your experience how does apartheid affect children's education?

2 On leaving school do all young people have the same opportunity to continue with sport?

3 In your particular sport, on what basis are teams chosen to represent South Africa?

4 Do you think the Olympic Movement is justified in excluding South Africa?

5 Do you believe it would be helpful if foreign teams played regularly in South Africa?

6 How do you feel about people like Sydney Maree, Zola Budd and others who have left South Africa to further their sporting careers?

7 What hope do you have for South African sport in the future?

The Minister for Women

AIMS

To gain knowledge and understanding of:

- the way women are discriminated against in sport
- the working of the Sex Discrimination Act
- the problems faced by women wishing to take part in leisure activities
- the activity patterns of women

To develop the skills of:

- formulating a questionnaire
- summarising and analysing arguments
- oral and written communication
- presenting data

 Assignment 1

Imagine you are the parliamentary private secretary for the Minister for Women. The following memorandum has just arrived for you, together with an extract from her speech, a summary of a leisure survey and two letters. Reply to the memo.

MEMORANDUM

From: S. Brown   To: PPS

Please let me have within two weeks your views and recommendations with regard to the implementation of the proposals I made in my recent speech, as attached. You may find the enclosed survey details on women and leisure to be of some use. Keep in mind the various opinions expressed by the pressure group who have written to me, and draft suitable replies.

'Woman of the Year' luncheon, 23rd October 1987 at the Waltdorf Hotel

From a speech given by the newly appointed Minister for Women, Ms Samantha Brown, on the role of women in sport.

. . . and it is, of course, essential that the world of sport is opened fully to women of all ages and interests. As I have already said, the attitude of men towards women, and indeed the attitude of women towards themselves, has changed considerably during this century. Today, if worthwhile physical activity is essential to men during their leisure hours, why should it not be so for women? If the husband can expect his wife to prepare his meal and put the children to bed while he plays squash, should she not be able to demand and receive equal treatment for her aerobics evening? Indeed, since, in practice, the majority of working wives do two jobs, a campaign of positive discrimination towards the participation of women in active leisure is necessary after a century of neglect. Sport and leisure activities are at present dominated and controlled by men to serve the needs of men. This must change. We need more women coaches, managers, trainers and above all administrators and directors. They alone have the power to direct resources and energy towards the needs of women. Women in sport at the moment are powerless. Like the magician's lady, they are merely a pretty diversion from the main act. The time for complaining is over. What we need now is action. The Sports Council, the CCPR and the governing bodies of sport must be made aware of the need to rid women of second-class status in sport and leisure. Further, we need research, conducted by women for women about the particular impact sport makes on their lives.

Finally, when equality of opportunity is given, a new pattern of achievement will emerge. No longer will women's performances be inferior to those of men. If the Badminton Three-Day Event can be won by a woman, why not the British Grand Prix? How long before a woman leads home the runners in the London marathon and we have a woman national snooker champion?

Dear Mrs Brown,

I really must draw your attention to an alternative view of the place of women, and indeed men also, in sport and leisure.

Frankly the pursuit of the body beautiful, the all-conquering competitor and the ego-enlarged participant are of little importance to a world full of problems. The energy expended in such ventures could be used for the good of society as a whole, both in this country and abroad. The victims of famine cry out to us, the lonely live and die without friends, the sick and those in trouble need our shoulders and our hearts. What should be our real priorities?

Yours sincerely,

Philippa Jones

The Everywhere Charity.

Dear Madam,

Let's get things straight about sport and stop beating about the bush. What Britain needs is winners. As in industry and commerce we must be number one. It doesn't matter how we get there, but we need and deserve that top spot. Now women have let us down badly in the past. Just look at the Wightman Cup record for instance. We need proper organisation and finance. It won't be cheap of course. All women must be tested to determine their potential. The lucky ones will be placed in schools for sport and we'll have champions, as many as you like. The rest of them will follow when we bring home the medals and our flag flies at the top. Can't think why it hasn't been done before.

Yours in sport,

Major George J. Trumpington (Ret.)
Chairman Consolidated Metal

1984 Survey by National Opinion Polls in Sheffield to investigate the leisure time of women

Number in sample: 707
Age range: 18–59 years
A range of social class backgrounds
A variety of residential areas

Findings

1 Restrictions on free time and leisure activities:
   – lack of time due to responsibility for housework and child care
   – lack of transport – not having access to a car and inconvenient public transport (linked to inability to move around freely after dark)
   – lack of money (reported by 64% of all women)

2 Activities undertaken during free time for the average week:

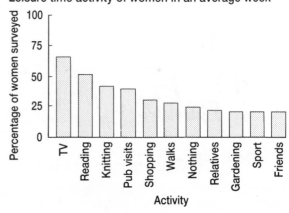

Leisure time activity of women in an average week

continued

---

3 The kinds of activities which women usually do are influenced by age, marital status, stage in the family cycle, income, social class and whether or not the woman is in paid work.

4 Of those playing sport, most of them did it once a week or more often. The most popular sports in order were swimming, badminton, tennis, running and squash. Participation was found to be particularly low amongst older women, working-class women and all women with a low income.

Assignment 2

As a group discuss the ways in which you might try to discover how women in your local community use their leisure time and also what their attitudes are towards active recreation.

You could produce a questionnaire. Consider the advice and guidelines given in the appendix, page 111.

You will need to gather the following information:

Personal: age, family situation, work
Transport: car, bicycle, public transport
Distance from facilities
Time spent on active recreations and activities undertaken
Reasons for taking part/not taking part in sport

You need to ensure that the sample of women used is representative of all the women in the community in terms of age, social class, residential area.

After completing all the interviews, collect the data and display your results visually (see appendix 2).

Analyse and discuss your results. Draw up a list of ways in which more women locally could be involved in active recreation. You might like to present them as part of a report to your local Sports Council.

Assignment 3

Sex discrimination in sport

Most people would agree that we should ensure fair play for all individuals involved in sport regardless of their sex. However, this is not the case. Sex discrimination is to be found throughout sport.

Example 1: Women are not allowed to compete at all in some athletic events – triple jump, pole vault, steeplechase, hammer throw.

Example 2: There is still a great deal of reluctance to accept women competing in such activities as rugby, wrestling, boxing, weightlifting, body building.

Example 3: Almost all sport is segregated into male-only and female-only competitions, even when there would appear to be no good reason (e.g. snooker, darts, rifle shooting, motor-racing).

If skill alone is considered, no woman at present deserves a place in an England football or cricket team. However, this should not mean that a woman should not be allowed to play for a club team if her ability alone makes her worth a place. At the prepubertal stage in junior schools, it would seem quite likely that many girls could compete on equal terms with boys in sport.

Discrimination against women competitors can be seen at all levels. They have fewer competitions, greater difficulty in training and inferior rewards compared with men. Further, most sports research has been conducted by men, on men, for men.

The Sex Discrimination Act

This Act makes it unlawful to discriminate on the grounds of sex in the general contexts of employment, education and the provision to the public of goods, services, premises and facilities. However, Section 44 of the Act exempts from the provision of the Act 'any sport, game or other activity of a competitive nature where the physical strength, stamina or physique of the average woman puts her at a disadvantage to the average man'.

Thus, sex discrimination in sport is currently preserved in law. A famous attempt to challenge this law was made by 11-year-old Theresa Bennett in 1978. She wanted to play football in the boys' youth team. It was claimed that she was worth a place in the team on ability alone. The Court of Appeal ruled against her, using Section 44 definitions. (That is, regardless of her particular ability, football is a game where the average woman is at a disadvantage compared with men, and therefore men may lawfully have men-only teams.) In athletics, the very best women marathon runners are able to beat the vast majority of men. Indeed, men and women usually run together but the results are separated. In some squash clubs, women and men players are completely integrated in leagues based entirely on merit. Discrimination does not exist in show-jumping and many other sports involving riding.

As a group discuss sex discrimination in sport, using the following starting points:

- If a sport accepts men should it not also accept women?
- Is society ready for women to box or for mixed-sex rugby teams?
- Should there be any limitations on participation in sport?

Summarise your views and present them in report form to the General Secretary of the CCPR, to be passed to the governing bodies of sport.

 Assignment 4

Sporting rewards

Wimbledon Tennis Championships 1987	Men	Women
Singles winner	£155,000	£139,500
Singles runner-up	£77,500	£69,750
Doubles winners (per pair)	£53,730	£46,500
Doubles runners-up (per pair)	£26,870	£23,250

1 Consider the above figures. Investigate other sports and see if a similar pattern emerges.

2 Imagine you are the women's champion in a sport where your reward is far inferior to that of the equivalent male champion. Write a letter to the organiser of your competition explaining why you believe your reward should be equivalent to that offered to the male champion.

 Assignment 5

Super Sally Snookered

Ever since she has been old enough to hold a cue, snooker has dominated Sally Knight's life. Her father Bill, a former amateur national champion, has developed her extraordinary talent and has shared her dream of being the best in the land.

Throughout her career she has practised and competed regularly with men and women. That is until last week. The bombshell that shattered her dream came when she was refused entry to the Electrika British Open Championships. Although she has all the qualifications required by the organisers, they have decided it is to be for men only. In their words – 'people don't want to watch some silly little girl draped all over the table'. They may also have in mind the fact that Sally was likely to pocket some of the £250,000 available in prize money. Bill Knight summed it all up by saying, 'What are they afraid of? Out on the table its only skill that counts – what does it matter if its a man or woman wearing the bow tie?'

Write a letter to the organisers of the championship explaining why you believe Sally Knight should be allowed to compete.

Assignment 6

Beryl Crockford Profile

34, formerly Beryl Mitchell,
Britain's top woman sculler.

Started rowing age 15 ■ First represented England in 1973 ■ Member of British team in first Olympics to include rowing (1976) ■ Silver medallist at 1981 World Championships ■ Reigning Champion of Women's Superstars ■ Qualified PE teacher, employed at Hammersmith & West London College.

Disadvantages Of Being A Woman . . . When I won the rowing prize at school, I wasn't given a tankard like the boys but a boring plaque. It annoyed me, not being treated the same, and it's something I've often come up against. It ranges from things like smaller changing rooms for women at sports centres to more important issues like having to use equipment designed for men, and the fact that the women's junior and senior teams get half the sponsorship money the men's senior team alone gets. As a woman I don't get as much recognition for my achievements, and that annoys me, since I make as many sacrifices for my sport as men. I once had to pay someone to do my job for the day while I rowed for my country.

From *Sport and Leisure*, July–August 1985

Consider your school, college, sports club or leisure centre and draw up a checklist to see if there are disadvantages in being a woman in sport. Here are a few examples to get you started:

- are all sports facilities available to both sexes?
- do both boys and girls learn the fundamental skills of the same activities?
- is equal publicity and kudos given to successful sportswomen and sportsmen?
- are all competitions open to both men and women?
- are mixed teams available in all sports?

Write a report suitable for presentation to the headmaster, principal or manager of the institution.

Sport reported

AIMS

To develop knowledge and understanding of:

- the extent to which sport has become part of our lives

- the effect of the media on our sporting knowledge and beliefs

- the qualities of a good sports reporter

- the way bias and personal interpretation can colour sports news

To develop the skills of:

- numeracy

- data collection and interpretation

- presenting informed judgements

- group work

Assignment 1

As a group collect a copy of each national newspaper printed on a particular day. For each newspaper find the total space allocated to sport. Count the lines in print and measure the pictures in square centimetres. Then divide the results for each newspaper into the space allocated to any particular sport. Copy and complete the following table for the group. Try to show your results in other visual forms such as bar graphs, pie charts etc. (see appendix 2).

SPORT	NEWSPAPERS					
	TIMES		MIRROR		EXPRESS	
	Print	Pictures	Print	Pictures	Print	Pictures
e.g.						
Football						
Rugby Union						
Horse racing						
TOTALS						
% of whole paper						

 Assignment 2

1 Consider how different newspapers treat the same sports story. Collect headlines, articles, reports and photographs to illustrate differences.

2 Do you think that the different approaches to sports reporting seen in various papers can be linked to those who buy the papers? Give reasons for your answer.

Why do you think there is no national daily sports paper to compare with *L'Equipe* in France? Get hold of a copy of *L'Equipe* and analyse its content. Perhaps your local newsagent will be able to order it for you. See if there are any differences between the way sport is reported in Britain and France. If you travel abroad you may be able to find out about sports reporting in other countries by looking at their newspapers.

 Assignment 3

Research by the Sports Council has found that the 20 most popular sports magazines in 1986 were as follows:

Sport	Magazine	Circulation (thousands)
Football	Shoot	200
Motor sports (2-wheeled)	Motor Cycle News	142
Golf	Golf News	140
Angling	Angling Times	115
Camping/caravanning	En Route (Caravan Club)	84
Angling	Anglers Mail	78
Motor sports (4-wheeled)	Motoring News	78
Golf	Golf World	74
Hunting/riding	Horse & Hound	73
Football	Match Weekly	70
Golf	Golf Monthly	68
Motor sports (4-wheeled)	Motor Sport	67
Motor sports (4-wheeled)	Motorist	67
Yachting	RYA News	65
Shooting	Shooting & Conservation	58
Athletics	Running Magazine	56
Yachting	Practical Boat Owner	54
Cycling	Cyclist Monthly	50
Riding	Horse and Pony	50
Shooting	Shooting Times and Country Magazine	47

Go to your nearest magazine retailer and obtain permission to list the sports magazines available. Try to find out the sales figures and compare your findings with those from other shops in your area investigated by others in your group and with the Sports Council's findings.

Construct a questionnaire to analyse the sports magazines read and/or bought by members of your group and compare the results you obtain with your other statistics.

Try to explain why some magazines are very popular and others less so. Is the most important factor the presentation of the sport or the sport itself?

Assignment 4

1   Attend a major sporting event which will be reported in national or local newspapers and write your own newspaper report, in advance of the printing of the newspapers. Collect a number of professional reports and compare and contrast them with your own. How do you account for such divergence of opinion?

2   List six qualities which you believe a good sports journalist should have.

Assignment 5

Although a journalist's main function is to report events as factually as possible, there will always be an element of personal interpretation.

In many countries reporting of events is controlled by the government. Winning at sport is very important to all nations today. Thus the way any particular international sports event is reported will depend on who is doing the reporting.

In the soccer World Cup 1986, the match between Argentina and England in which Maradona scored a controversial goal was very differently reported by the two countries.

The following report suggests how differently Britain and Australia treated Australia's Davis Cup victory and Ashes defeat in 1986.

Wizards of Oz tennis conjure away Ashes' loss

From Martin Johnson in Melbourne

IF THE Baron de Coubertin had ever made his Olympic speech in Australia, he would have been a strong candidate for a strait-jacket and a padded cell. Here, it's not the taking part, it's the winning.

Only the most dogged search in yesterday's newspapers managed to un-earth the fact that England's cricketers had retained the Ashes, while a routine perusal of the front pages left no one in any doubt that Pat Cash is a warm favourite to become the first Australian Pope.

Only eight kilometres and 47 minutes separated Australia's Davis Cup tennis victory at Kooyong and their Fourth Test defeat at the MCG, which sent the nation into almost simultaneous delight and despair. Cash's prize was an overnight move in "Good on yer Pat" tee-shirts and an official reception with the Prime Minister, while just down the road "Clashes for the Ashes" souvenir hats were being blown around the Melbourne pavements.

The PM managed to tear himself away from Pat just long enough to offer a few consoling words to Allan Border's lads:

"The less said the better. What a disaster."

In a way, it was remarkable that the cricket rated a mention at all. Bad sporting news is usually withheld on the grounds that it could damage national morale.

However, tucked away beneath interviews with Pat's tennis racquet, the Australian press delivered its verdict on the team that batted for eight-and-a-half hours in two innings against a below strength attack on an undemanding pitch. "Gutless" and "Spineless" were two of the kinder observations.

From the *Independent*, 30 December 1986

Use the following information to write a report in
biased form for home consumption of either nation

Match:
Soccer World Cup qualifying round, first leg.

Teams:
Home side: 'Zagaland', used to playing on their hard pitches in
cold weather. Traditional physical approach to the game.

Away side: 'Mindidi', used to playing on wet pitches in hot weather.
Traditional artistic approach to the game.

The game:
Mindidi found conditions difficult for the first 20 minutes and were
on the defensive. They conceded 10 corners in this period, their
goalkeeper made 2 very good saves and one shot was headed
off the goal line. Although Zagaland made a number of other
chances in the rest of the half, most shots were off target.

Mindidi gradually improved their performance, looking
increasingly dangerous in attack. In the 40th minute they hit the
post and in the following mêlée were awarded a penalty. They
scored only after it had been retaken because the referee ruled
the goalkeeper had moved too early in saving the first shot.

The second half opened with Zagaland on the defensive. Against
the run of play they equalised when a back pass to the
goalkeeper was intercepted. They improved their play, taking the
lead when from a corner an unchallenged forward headed into an
open goal.

The Mindidi goalkeeper was injured at this corner and taken to
hospital (65 mins). For the rest of the game play was even, the
best chances falling to Mindidi with the Zagaland goalkeeper
making one outstanding save.

Result: 2–1 to Zagaland.

Second leg in six weeks' time.

Assignment 6

The names of some sports commentators have
become inseparable from the sport on which they
commentate. Eddie Waring was an outstanding
example, as this tribute shows.

Eddie, the voice of rugby league

**PAUL RYLANCE pays
tribute to rugby league
commentator Eddie Waring,
who died yesterday**

EDDIE WARING, the jaunty,
cheerful chappie who became
the controversial symbol of rugby league during a 30-year career as the BBC's commentator
of the game, died yesterday in a
nursing home near Leeds at the
age of 76, leaving his widow and
one son.

Mr Waring, who also became a
popular presenter of
television's *It's a Knockout*, suffered a stroke soon after his retirement four years ago and
never fully recovered.

His quixotic tilts with the English
language on Saturday after-
noons made him almost a cult
figure and catchphrases like
"up and under", "early bath"
and "he's a big lad", are still
very much in use throughout
the land.

But his presentation of the game
also brought criticism from
within. He was accused in some
quarters of trivialising the game
to the point of being a joke, but
those who knew him will testify
that this was not his intention.
No one loved the game more,
no one lived for the game like
he did and no one put more
into it.

Whatever one feelings, it cannot
be denied that he was charis-
matic and because of his engag-
ing appeal to television viewers,
rugby league was able to shed
its parochial mantle and gain
national recognition.

But beneath the famous tilted tril-
by was a man of passion and a
pioneer. At the age of 26, he
became the youngest adminis-
trator in the game as secretary
of Dewsbury before moving to
Headingley as manager of
Leeds. He launched himself
into journalism as the rugby

league correspondent of the
Sunday Pictorial and later with
the *Sunday Mirror*.

He was the presenter when rugby
league was first launched on
BBC television in 1951 with the
screening of the Test match between Great Britain and New
Zealand at Swinton.

But behind the scenes he did not
rest. Bleak nights he travelled
far and wide in Lancashire,
Yorkshire and Cumbria with
his road-show of rugby films,
quizzes and auctions which
raised a fortune for charity.

David Oxley, the Leeds' Secretary
General, said yesterday: "Eddie had his critics, but they did
not know him. Rugby league
was his life and no one has done
more for the game. He had tre-
mendous energy and enthusiasm and when he wasn't working he was rushing about raising
money for charity. He will be
greatly missed."

Ray French, the St Helens school-
master who took over the rugby
commentaries for the BBC,
said: "Having to follow Eddie
was a heck of a job. He had become a cult figure and the more
outrageous his remarks the
more people loved him, but on

the two programmes I shared
with him he was marvellous in
helping me to overcome my
nerves.

"I would never knock him. He was
a great character and brought
the game to many new areas.
He made people aware of rugby league for the first time."

Bill Cotton, the managing director of BBC television, said: "To
BBC viewers, Eddie Waring
was the voice of Rugby League
for many years."

From the *Independent*, 29 October 1986

Complete this list with the names of commentators which you most readily associate with each sport.

Sport	Commentator(s)
Rugby league	Eddie Waring
Rugby union	
Athletics	
Tennis	
Golf	
Soccer	
Darts	
Snooker	
Motor racing	

Make a tape recording of your favourite commentator in action. Consider the qualities of a good commentator, how the event is better conveyed to the audience and the importance of the commentator's individual style and particular use of language. Write your own tribute in approximately 300 words.

What price excellence?

AIMS

To increase knowledge and understanding of:

- the factors which contribute to sporting success

- the drive and dedication essential for successful top-class sporting performance

- the stresses and strains associated with trying to be the best

- how successful sportsmen and sportswomen cope with the pressures of sport at the top

- the fleeting quality of a sporting career

To develop the skills of:

- comprehension

- analysis

- written and oral communication

- information retrieval

Champion material

To be a champion you need a combination of natural talent, hard work and a little luck! Of course there are many other factors which are also important – the interest of parents, type of education, financial security, local environment and facilities, personality, good health and many others.

Assignment 1

Do different sports require different proportions of all the factors mentioned on page 97? Copy out and complete the following table and add three others of your choice. You have 100 marks in total to award for each person.

Have any patterns emerged in your marks to ·suggest that one quality is more important for success than others? Use the information to draw a bar graph, or a pie chart (see appendix 2).

100 marks total per competitor

SPORT	INDIVIDUAL	Natural talent	Effort in performance	Effort in training	Personality	Others
(a) Tennis	M. Navratilova					
(b) Snooker	S. Davis					
(c) Soccer	B. Robson					
(d) Ice dance	J. Torvill					
(e) Athletics (Decathlon)	D. Thompson					
(f) Squash	J. Khan					
(g) Athletics (Javelin)	F. Whitbread					
(h)						
(i)						
(j)						
	Average					

 Assignment 2

Read the following article and write answers to the questions which follow:

Asthmatic Achievers

An occasional series on notable people of our time who have fought against asthma — and won!
Adrian Moorhouse, MBE, Captain of British Swimming Team.
Adrian Moorhouse describes his experiences in his own words:

I've had asthma since I was very young and bronchial asthma I believe was my particular 'variety'. My father was very sports inclined, so I was given every opportunity of following almost any sport, rugby and cricket being the sports at school. I found it hard to make the full game of rugby, also I couldn't run a lap of the track without being badly out of breath, but I found that swimming didn't affect me like this. Since I was eight I was winning local championships and breaking school records. I remember one school swimming championships, however, when I was really bad and had been in bed off school for a week. I believe it was 1976. I was determined to be the Victor Aquarum — and that meant winning so many races, as I missed the first three races the week before. I got there anyway with my spinhaler and managed to pull it off.

It's quite hard to explain my condition really, regarding swimming, because I was never as bad as some of my friends. However, quite occasionally it would knock me out. Even now if I get a bad cold it goes on to my chest and that's training gone for a week, but when I'm really fit I don't usually have any problems.

I really owe the fact that I kept up swimming to a Specialist I saw when I was about 12. I was having problems with athletics and he told me to keep on swimming training as it would do me the most good. I don't know how much of his advice was true medically — but at that time it was psychologically the best thing that could have happened to me. I kept training hard, and even if it got bad I thought that it was doing me some good. I don't know if I grew out of my condition, or if the training helped to make me breathe easier — but now I don't have many problems. I think one of the most pleasing things which swimming did for me was when I did a half marathon run (13½ miles) in 1985 — it gave me so much satisfaction when I remember how I used to struggle around the school track. Running is easier now — I didn't do it as a one-off thing — although I don't use running in my training. When I am out of season I do up to ten miles a week (October-November). It's quite hard on my breathing at first, but the more I do, the easier it gets.

I don't think that asthma has interfered with my ambition at all, because I haven't let it. I just kept on training. I suppose it made me more determined, because at school I was never going to get on the athletics team or the rugby team, so just to prove that I could do something as well as the other kids — swimming was the way to do it.·

From *Asthma News*, No. 15, 15 July 1987

1 Why did Adrian Moorhouse take up swimming?

2 What is asthma? Try to find out if you are unsure.

3 Why is asthma likely to cause problems for sportsmen and sportswomen?

4 Do you know anyone who is asthmatic? How does asthma affect their daily life? Are they able to take part in sport? Give details if you can.

5 Should people with medical problems take part in sport? Could they be building up problems for the future?

6 International swimmers usually train in the water at least twice a day. Would you be prepared to give up this amount of time to a sport? Are there other things that you would rather do?

7 What qualities of personality has Adrian Moorhouse shown in overcoming his problem?

8 What do you think he has gained from his sporting success?

 Assignment 3

Read the following article and write answers to the questions which follow.

JOANNE CONWAY cut an indelible picture on our television screens last week. In defending her British title she proved not only that she was out on her own as a figure skater, but also a champion hardened far beyond her 15 years.

The traces of adolescence were few. The sureness on ice was unnervingly mature. Off camera, the youngest champion British ice skating has produced in 30 years, *is* a child, but one driven by extraordinary determination to be best.

She has two sets of adults, two pairs of guardians, virtually beholden to her dream. Tom and Miriam Conway in North Shields, ordinary working parents with two ordinary career-minded older children, are sacrificing 99% of their daughter's time and their financial security to put her into a coaching school 4,000 miles away. In Colorado Springs, Carlo and Christa Fassi, trainers to four world champions, are propelling her towards fame and perhaps a distant fortune.

Failure is unthinkable. The girl will not have it, any more than at 11 she would accept a surgeon's advice that she should never compete again after another skater's blade accidentally sliced through her Achilles tendon. "I will not give in," she replied. "I will never give in." . . .

The Fassis took to Joanne for one reason: "She has the talent," says Christa.

Tom and Miriam Conway [find that] trusting their daughter's welfare and upbringing to others is a terrible wrench. "It's worst when she has to go to the doctor's," says Miriam, "and we can't be there."

Besides the Fassis there is a personal academic tutor. Tom would be happier if she could be integrated into a proper school but he reasons: "It's not so important, being a girl, is it? She's not going to be a breadwinner.". . .

The Conway dilemma is not how far to push their daughter, but how they could live with denying her opportunity. . . . No one can take from her triumphs achieved and places visited at the tender age of 15. But no one can give her back her childhood.

From *The Sunday Times*, 30 November 1986

1   Explain why Joanne's life is not normal for a 15-year-old.

2   What special strain is this lifestyle likely to put on a young person?

3   Would you be prepared to make such sacrifices for possible future reward?

4   Why do you think her parents are willing to let her live this way?

5   Do you think she is missing out on anything other girls of her own age would get?

6   Could sport be so important that you would be prepared to sacrifice everything for success?

7   Imagine that she is unable to get home to see her family for Christmas because she needs to train for a championship in the New Year. Write a letter from her mother or father explaining how you feel about her decision.

8   Is her father right about the fact that she does not go to a proper school when he says 'It's not so important, being a girl, is it? She's not going to be a bread winner.'

Assignment 4

Soon forgotten

In modern times many thousands of sportsmen and sportswomen have made sacrifices in their search for sporting success. Of them only a relatively small number have made any impact at national level. Fewer still have achieved lasting success. Fame for most is both limited and fleeting.

1   Test this for yourself by trying to name the sporting achievement associated with the following who received national acclaim in Britain in the post-war years. If you get stuck your Mum or Dad will probably be able to help!

1	Stirling Moss	11	Beryl Burton
2	Christine Trueman	12	Mary Peters
3	Freddie Trueman	13	Jonah Barrington
4	Duncan Edwards	14	Colin Cowdrey
5	Mike Hailwood	15	Gareth Edwards
6	Derek Ibbotson	16	Clare Francis
7	Randolf Turpin	17	David Wilkie
8	Mary Rand	18	Brian Phelps
9	Tony Jacklin	19	Sharron Davies
10	Pat Smythe	20	Lillian Board

2   Can you name ten different sportsmen or sportswomen who achieved fame in different sports before the Second World War? Try to give their nationality and brief details of their claim to fame.

3   Explain why the feats of sportsmen and sportswomen are so quickly forgotten. Is the same true of people who write music or books, or who win wars or explore or invent? What ensures that a person's name is remembered far beyond the event and their lifetime?

Assignment 5

Coping with success

A few British sports stars have, through their personal qualities and approach to sport, found a special place in the affection of the nation.

1   Try to complete the following roll of honour and add any additional names to the list which you think would be suitable.

For Outstanding Qualities in the field of Sport the following have been awarded a place on the Roll of Honour

Bobby Charlton: *Skill of the highest order, scrupulous fair play, sportsmanship and modesty.*

Henry Cooper:

Virginia Wade:

Mary Peters:

Bill Beaumont:

Success in any walk of life brings its own pressures and stress. In the sporting world success often comes quickly to young people. Not all superstars have found it easy to cope.

In the '60s George Best, star of Manchester United and Northern Ireland, had the world at his feet. He was the proud owner of a string of shops, lived in an expensive house and moved with the famous. His decline as a footballer was accompanied by financial and personal problems.

More recently John McEnroe's attitude to officials and opponents on court and the press and public off court earned him the title 'Superbrat'. Alex 'Hurricane' Higgins's behaviour at a number of tournaments has brought condemnation throughout a sport renowned for its exemplary sporting behaviour. Ian Botham in his role as a 'Sporting Cavalier' has found himself at odds with the cricket authorities and has regularly provided the press with a succession of lurid headlines.

2 Imagine you are the coach/manager/trainer of a very talented young sportsman or sportswoman who is often in trouble with referees, umpires and officials in general. Draw up a list of 'Do's' and 'Don'ts' which you believe might help to keep him or her out of trouble.

 Assignment 6

Sporting pressures

Some professional sports offer vast sums of money to the most successful players, but demand a lifestyle which for many is not sustainable. An example is the professional tennis circuit. With world-wide competitions throughout the year, even the stars find they are travelling and living out of a suitcase for much of the year.

The five-times Wimbledon Champion Bjorn Borg decided that, at the age of 26, he had had enough and retired. John McEnroe, his successor, found that he needed a long break from tennis to develop his life in other directions. For junior up-and-coming players the demands are just as great with very few achieving the rewards of stardom. In such a demanding career the only thing that matters is success on the court.

The physical demands made on young players is a cause for concern, especially young women who compete in top tennis tournaments before they are 15. Persistent injuries have forced young stars such as Andrea Jaeger and Tracy Austin to retire while still in their teens. Other sports where young female competitors would seem to be at risk are gymnastics, swimming and athletics.

Imagine you are the parent of an exceptionally talented daughter aged 10 who is tipped as a future champion. Write a letter to the governing body of her sport explaining your worries about her future health – physical and mental – if she continues with her chosen sport to the highest level.

Assignment 7

Opponents

The respect that competitors have for their rivals is derived from a number of sources. These include the personality of the competitor, the way he or she has been encouraged to think of rivals, and the demands made by their trainers and coaches.

Some people argue that in today's ultra-competitive world it is impossible for competitors to have a close and friendly relationship with those they seek to defeat. They say that the higher a sportsman or sportswoman moves up the ladder of success, the greater the investment in success in terms of effort, time and money, so concern for rivals is a distraction which cannot be afforded.

Others would say that if all feelings for an opponent are lost, then sport is deprived of its essentially human value.

Consider the following comments. Try to decide who made them and which sport is involved. Could they be said to reflect an amateur or professional attitude? Would you agree with them?

At 6ft 2ins and 13st, ▮▮▮▮ in full flight is an intimidating sight and his tongue, which moves as fast as his feet, is just as forceful. After Europe, it's the world, he says. "Being the best in Europe is not enough. I want to be the greatest ▮▮▮ ever."

"▮ is out to beat me and I'm going to make sure that doesn't happen. It is a case of kill or be killed, eat or be eaten.

"It is like boxing in that if you don't believe in yourself it's no go. ▮▮▮▮ is 40 per cent getting the mental attitude right and psyching yourself up.

"But, unlike boxers, I couldn't give an opponent a cuddle after he had been trying to beat out my brains. I hate the guys I ▮ against. I shake their hands after the ▮▮, never before, out of respect, but that doesn't mean to say I have to like them.

"I want to be the best and if I can't it hurts. When I lose, I'm not happy and don't want to speak to anyone. If I gave an interview, it would look as if I was content with coming second."

From the *Independent*, 23 January 1987

Assignment 8

Sports stars are often quoted in the press. Make up a collection of quotes of the week, or month or year. Here are some of the more famous quotes of 1987:

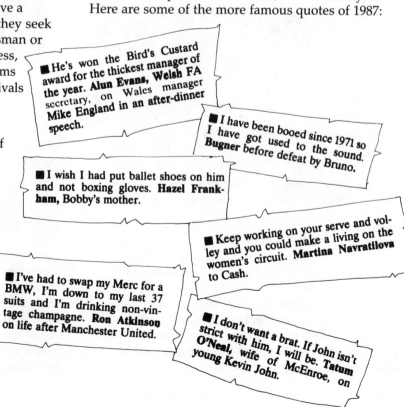

Outdoor pursuits

AIMS

To gain knowledge and understanding of:

- the attractions of outdoor pursuits
- the dangers of natural hazards
- the precautions needed when taking part in outdoor activities
- the necessity for an adequate diet when facing natural hazards
- first aid

To develop the skills of:

- comprehension
- communication
- problem-solving
- planning diets

 ## Assignment 1

I found a friend of the family who did a little climbing and he took me to Harrison Rocks, a small outcrop of sandstone just south of London. It wasn't ten metres high. You climbed with the protection of a rope hitched round one of the many trees at the top of the crag. At the end of the day, I knew that I had found something I was good at and loved doing. The basic satisfaction of climbing is both physical and mental – a matter of co-ordination similar to any other athletic attachment. But in climbing there is the extra ingredient of risk. It is a hot, heady spice, a piquance that adds an addictive flavour to the game.

It is accentuated by the fascination of pitting one's ability against a personal unknown and winning through. Being master of one's destiny, with one's life literally in one's hands, is what gives climbing its fascination. It also gives a heightened awareness of everything around. The pattern of lichen on rock, a few blades of grass, the dark, still shape of a lake below, the form of the hills and the cloud mountains above might be the same view seen by the passengers on a mountain railway, but transported to his viewpoint amongst a crowd, he cannot see what I, the climber, can.

Quest for Adventure, Chris Bonington

1 Explain in your own words why Chris Bonington finds climbing so attractive.

2 What do you think he means by saying that the satisfaction is both physical and mental?

3 How important to him is it that in climbing he risks his life? Are you attracted to activities which have an element of risk?

4 Completing a climb obviously gives a feeling of achievement. Can you suggest achievements in other sports which would give similar feelings?

5 Do you think it is true that climbers see the world differently from those remaining on the ground below?

6 Climbing is generally thought of as a non-competitive activity. Are there any ways in which it might be considered competitive?

 Assignment 2

The diver

I put on my aqualung and plunge,
Exploring, like a ship with a glass keel,
The secrets of the deep. Along my lazy road
On and on I steal –
Over waving bushes which at a touch explode
Into shrimps, then closing rock to the tune of the
        tide;
Over crabs that vanish in puffs of sand.
Look, a string of pearls bubbling at my side
Breaks in my hand –
Those pearls were my breath . . .! Does that hollow
        hide
Some old Armada wreck in seaweed furled,
Crusted with barnacles, her cannon rusted,
The great *San Philip*? What bullion in her hold?
Pieces of eight, silver crowns, and bars of solid
        gold?
I shall never know. Too soon the clasping cold
Fastens on flesh and limb
And pulls me to the surface. Shivering, back I swim
To the beach, the noisy crowds, the ordinary world.

Ian Serraillier

1 What does the diver enjoy about diving in this poem?

2 Many outdoor activities involve exploring the unknown. Why do you think some people find the unknown so attractive?

3 The diver talks about getting cold. Why is this likely to be a problem? Find out what other dangers there are for sub-aqua divers and what precautions should be taken by those involved?

4 What does the last line tell you about the way the diver feels about the world beneath the waves and the real world up above?

5 Try to write a short poem about an outdoor activity which you have experienced. Try to remember the impact it had on you and convey these feelings. You may be able to find some other poems about outdoor activities.

Assignment 3

1   How do people get involved in outdoor pursuits? Is it usually through their family like Chris Bonington? How important are schools and voluntary groups in introducing young people? If a friend of yours wanted to know how to take up canoeing or parascending, what advice would you give about how to get started?

2   Make a list of all the outdoor activities that you can think of. Tick those that you have tried, put a circle around those that you would like to try and put a cross against any you are not interested in. Collect this information together for your group and display your results in a visual form (see appendix 2).

3   Against each activity in your list, name the organisation responsible for the activity in this country. Make notes about the way each activity is run, controlled and financed. Find out the responsibilities, if any, of the Government, local authority, Sports Council and CCPR. To what extent, if any, is private enterprise involved?

To answer these questions fully you may need to consult your local library and the Sports Council.

Assignment 4

```
                                                  'Fallen Arches',
                                                  Longshaw,
                                                  Near Southminster,
                                                  Essex

                                                  29th October


Mr R. Flowers,
Westbury Outdoor Pursuits Centre,
Hay-on Wye,
HEREFORDSHIRE

Dear Mr Flowers,

      Congratulations on your appointment as Warden of Warren Park Farm Activities
Centre.  I am very pleased that you have accepted the post and I look forward to
many years of working together to ensure the success of the centre.

A number of problems need resolving before the courses start in March next year.
I have enclosed a memo and information which you need to respond to within the next
four weeks.

Please do not hesitate to contact me regarding any of the above matters.  I will
be out of the country until the 3rd November, but after that date I will be readily
accessible.

                                    Yours sincerely,

                                    M. Malone

                                    Molly Malone.
```

MEMORANDUM

To: R. Flowers   From: Flonie Bunda   Date: 26 October

As you know, Ron Bund, who has just left the centre for a new post in Scotland, was responsible for publicity and bookings as well as being the assistant warden. He had intended to create some new publicity material to send out to primary and secondary schools early in the new year. Obviously this has not been done and so I wonder if you could draw up some leaflets and application forms which we could distribute?

I have attached some basic information about the centre including the range of activities which are possible.

Warren Park Farm Activities Centre
Longshaw
Southminster
Essex
Tel. Longshaw 1214

Warren Park Farm was purchased in 1974 by the Charitable Knowsley Youth Trust and has since been transformed into a well-equipped outdoor pursuits centre.

It now contains bunk dormitories for 30 young people, lounge, well-equipped kitchen, gymnasium, showers and drying room.

There is a small farm run in conjunction with the centre which can provide practical opportunities for any interested youngster, e.g. milking, butter making, animal husbandry.

The main activities include canoeing (double kayaks and Canadian open canoeing), sailing (small dinghys), campcraft, orienteering, navigation, night expedition, recreational games and initiative tests.

In addition life saving instruction is included with the chance of obtaining a national award at a basic level.

All participants must be able to swim and be prepared to attempt all the activities.

Length of courses 3–12 days. Age range 13–16 years.

Respond to the letter by preparing the following:

(i) An A4 leaflet advertising the benefits of a course at the centre.
(ii) A more detailed form showing the courses on offer as well as an application form.
(iii) A 30-second promotional advert designed to go on the local radio.

You should assume that you will have three full-time members of staff who are qualified to undertake the complete range of outdoor pursuits you currently have on offer.

You also have two part-time odd-job men who look after the grounds and all of the equipment.

The centre transport consists of two Land Rovers and three trailers suitable for ferrying the canoes.

 ## Assignment 5

MEMORANDUM		
From: R. Flowers	To: Mollie Malone	Date: 30 October

As was made clear at your pre-interview visit to the Centre, relationships with the local community have deteriorated over the last two years. The most recent incident which involved a number of students being seen bathing nude in the village pond at 11.30 at night, did nothing to help the situation.

In an attempt to establish a more friendly climate I have arranged a meeting between the centre management and some representatives from the parish council. This meeting will take place on 4th November in the village hall at 8 p.m. and the management committee would like you to attend. I think that it is important that we have answers to the following points:

1) The value of residential experience for young people.
2) How activities at the centre could contribute to the life of the village.
3) How we will ensure that students do not abuse the village and its surroundings.

Additionally, it would be advisable to have responses ready to the points raised in the letters attached.

M. Malone

Prepare replies to the questions raised in the memo above.

Dear Mrs. Malone,

     I wish to express the strongest of objections to the continued use of Warren Park Farm as an Outdoor Pursuit Centre. I have been a resident of Longshaw, man and boy for some seventy five years and base my objections on the following points.

(1) Longshaw has always been a peaceful, secluded village. The sudden influx of 30-40 young people with too much energy, too much money and too little self control has changed the whole nature of the village. No longer is it safe for villagers to sit and talk on the village green. I myself have been almost hit by a base ball and our chance of winning a prize for the best kept village in Essex has disappeared under a pile of litter.

(2) Even our nights are not sacred. I have witnessed groups of your students trekking through the village in the small hours of the morning, seemingly without adequate adult supervision.

(3) Our local fishing club object to the use of the river for canoeing. What was once a prime fishing site deteriorated to a noisy dirty and polluted area

I could raise many other points. The most important point to underline, however, is that no outsider, however well intentioned, should be able to descend onto our village and spoil it for residents such as myself.

Yours faithfully

Montague Wilberforce (Admiral of the Fleet, Retired)

Assignment 6

Emergencies

All active leisure pursuits carry an element of risk. In outdoor activities there are many additional dangers due entirely to the nature of the activities.

Those responsible for groups of people taking part are well aware of the dangers and every precaution is taken both before setting out and during the activity. When accidents do occur a well-rehearsed rescue operation swings into action.

Consider the following incidents.

INCIDENT A

Group:	Ten 13/14-year-olds, mixed, novices.
Staff:	Leader and assistant leader in canoes.
Activity:	Canoeing in slalom canoes.
Place:	Slow-flowing river, 30m wide, winding, largely tree lined.
Month:	November.
Time:	3.30 p.m.
Weather:	Light wind, sudden deterioration, fierce gusts and driving rain, cold.

Incident:

The group has been canoeing for an hour, after two hours on the water in the morning. Canoeing one behind the other they follow the assistant leader with the leader in the rear. The sudden squall capsizes the assistant leader and three other canoes. He is seen unharmed on the surface towing his canoe but without a paddle. Three others of the group are in the water, one is clinging to her canoe and being swept ahead of the group out of sight around the next bend. Two other canoeists are in the water, one seemingly unconscious with a cut forehead, the other swimming with his canoe to the bank. The rest of the group are afloat but badly shaken and in disarray.

INCIDENT B

Group:	Twenty-five 10-year-olds, mixed, from the junior section of the local youth club.
Staff:	A leader and two adult assistants.
Activity:	Walking and nature study.
Place:	A large forest.
Month:	July.
Weather:	Very hot.

Incident:

After leisurely walking for an hour and a half an early lunch is taken in a clearing, as a number of the group are complaining of headaches and dizziness. They are thirsty but unable to eat their lunch. During the rest two other children creep away and climb a tree. A sudden scream reveals one child lying under the tree with both legs obviously broken and the other white with fright and shaking 10m above the ground. Whilst these two are being attended to the whole group is quickly called together. A roll call shows two children missing.

INCIDENT C

Group:	Five experienced hill walkers.
Staff:	Group includes a fully qualified leader.
Activity:	50-mile walk with two overnight stops.
Place:	Fell country.
Month:	April.
Time:	Second day, 17.00 hours.
Weather:	Very cold and clear.

Incident:

Just before preparing to stop for the night on the second day, the two leading walkers slip 5m down a gully. The first has a badly swollen ankle and is completely unable to put any weight on it. The second has sustained cuts to knees, hands and face which are bleeding badly. As these two are being treated, snow starts to fall and visibility is rapidly reduced to a few metres.

Imagine you are the group leader; prepare a report about each incident for the centre manager.
Consider the following questions in your report:

1 What safety precautions were taken before the activity?
Take into account the:

- experience and fitness of the group
- instructions given to individuals and the group as a whole
- weather conditions
- equipment issued and whether it was checked

2 What action was taken when the accident occurred?
Take into account the:

- seriousness of personal injury (if any)
- immediate danger for some or all of the group (if any)
- loss or damage to equipment
- means of summoning outside help
- method of returning group to base
- prevailing or changing weather conditions

 Assignment 7

Diet

Outdoor activities are very demanding physically. Apart from being fit for the activity in the first place, participants must receive an adequate food supply if they are to be able to meet the demands of the activity.

The main constituents of a diet are as follows:

Carbohydrates .... provide energy
Proteins .... build and repair the body
Fats .... long-term energy store
Vitamins .... regulate body activity
Minerals .... essential for well-being
Water .... vital for life

When deciding on what food to eat during an activity a number of important factors have to be considered including:

- does the food have to be carried during the activity?
- will it satisfy hunger?
- does it have to be cooked or heated?
- does it require water to cook or reconstitute it?
- will it deteriorate quickly?
- does it require utensils to prepare it?
- how long does it take to prepare?
- is it easily packed?

Bearing in mind the above points, give meal plans and general food advice for the following activities. You may find it helpful to refer to a book on diet to find out exactly what everyday foodstuffs contain in terms of protein, carbohydrates etc.

1 A cold, packed lunch for an adult sailing group to eat ashore in a hut with no cooking facilities.

2 Lunch, evening meal and breakfast for an overnight canoe camping group of 15/16-year-olds leaving base at 10 a.m. one day and returning at 11.00 a.m. the next day. The group must be self-sufficient.

3 Lunch and an early evening light meal for three mountain walkers leaving after breakfast and returning at nightfall in summer with good weather conditions.

4 Menus for four people for 5 days on a narrowboat in October, cruising on inland waterways. Daily supplies of bread and milk are available from lock keepers.

5 Basic emergency provisions for a mountain hut which may be used by walkers and climbers in severe weather. These supplies should be enough for two weeks' survival.

6 A seven-day single-handed yacht race around Britain has been organised to see which boat can be sailed the furthest from a named port. You have entered. List the food supplies you would consider necessary for the race.

How to obtain facts and information

A number of the assignments ask you to obtain information from a variety of sources, to analyse the information you obtain and finally to display your analysis in an effective manner.

There are many ways of obtaining information. We will look in detail at the following:

Questionnaires
Interviews
Observation and experimentation
Secondary data

Questionnaires

A questionnaire consists of a series of appropriate questions designed to give you the information you are seeking. It is particularly useful when you want to find out what a large number of people feel, know or do.

For example:
'Attempt to find out how students in your year at school or college spend their leisure time.'

Decide first whether the questionnaire is to be **self-completion** (filled in by the respondents themselves) or whether you or a friend is going to interview the respondents (**a structured interview**).

Self-completion questionnaires

Self-completion questionnaires save a lot of interviewing time and so usually allow you to obtain information from a much larger number of people. The questions asked have to be very simple and straightforward as there is no opportunity to explain them to the respondent.

The information you get back is less reliable, particularly if you have asked questions about attitudes or beliefs. The main problem however is actually getting people to fill in written questionnaires and return them to you.

There are two main categories of questions: **closed** (pre-coded) and **open** questions.

Closed questions

In this type of question a list of answers is supplied. The respondent is normally asked to choose one of the possible answers.

For example:
How many hours a week do you normally spend in sporting activities? (Tick one)

Up to 1 hour	0	☐
Up to 2 hours	1	☐
Up to 3 hours	2	☐
Up to 4 hours	3	☐
Up to 5 hours	4	☐
Up to 6 hours	5	☐
Above 6 hours	6	☐

Closed questions are quicker to fill in and quicker to analyse, but they may force respondents to choose categories which do not represent their true position and they don't necessarily enable you to find out what the respondent really thinks.

Open questions

Open questions are those where the answers are so numerous that they cannot be written on the question paper.

For example:
'What improvements would you make to the leisure facilities in your immediate neighbourhood if you had the resources?'

Open questions are better for finding out what people really think and the answers are always in their own words. However, some respondents will always write very little, and the results can be difficult to analyse on a large scale.

Open questions are useful if you are not familiar with the group being questioned and cannot be confident that you can choose the right closed responses.

It is often a good idea to include both closed and open questions in a questionnaire. Apart from obtaining different sorts of information it also makes the questionnaire more interesting to complete.

How to construct a self-completion questionnaire

1   Decide exactly what you want to know from your questionnaire. Some possibilities based on the example above are:

- the amount of time left for leisure activities each week
- whether leisure patterns are different for the sexes
- the cost of leisure activities etc.

2   Write out questions in rough which ask for answers to the above list. Avoid questions which are:

(a) ambiguous
'How much time do you have left once you have finished your work?'
It is not clear what 'work' covers – does it just mean college work or does it include housework or any part-time employment the student might have? It is also not clear what particular time period is being mentioned, i.e. one day, one week, one year.

(b) long and complicated

'Once you have finished your college work, completed all of your home chores such as washing, cooking etc. and also finished your part-time work if you have any, how much time do you have left? Do not include travelling time and sleeping time.'

(c) leading
'Students don't have enough free time, do they?'

(d) embarrassing
'How many hours a week do you spend with your girlfriend/boyfriend?'

Remember all questions should be

- short
- clear and simple
- unambiguous

The sort of questions you write should depend on the type of information you are seeking.

3 Try your questionnaire on a few of your friends. See if they respond to the questions in the way you hoped. Change the wording of questions which appear to confuse and include new ones if certain necessary information is not forthcoming.

4 Produce a finished version of your questionnaire. Make sure that it is clearly printed and easy to read. Space out the questions and allow sufficient room for respondents to write their answers.

Be sure to include an introduction which explains who you are and why you are seeking information from them.

5 You must decide who is going to complete the questionnaires. It would almost certainly be too expensive in both time and money to include all students in the year and so you will have to select a sample.

You would be likely to get a biased picture if you only asked all students on the Sports and Leisure Course to complete the questionnaire. It would be sensible to obtain a stratified random sample. Do this by getting hold of separate lists of all male and female students in your year. Give each student a number. Use a table of random numbers (from your maths teacher or lecturer) in order to select the desired number of male and the desired number of female students.

6 Issue the questionnaires to the selected group of students and arrange for them to complete the questionnaire and for you to collect them.

7 Collect the questionnaires and analyse the answers to each question. The closed questions can probably be presented in statistical form (see appendix 2).

8 Use the results you have obtained in order to make some general findings about the topic you have investigated.

Interviews

Structured interviews

You could also find the answers to the question by carrying out structured interviews. The same questions could be used but this time the questions are asked by the interviewer. The interviewer is able to develop questions and ensure answers are given more fully than would be the case with the self-completion questionnaire.

Time must be allowed for each interview and so it may not be possible to obtain information from as large a number of students as with a self-completion questionnaire.

In-depth interviews

If you want to get very detailed information from a small number of people, then conducting in-depth interviews is probably the most effective means.

For example:
'Interview an ex-sportsman or sportswoman and try to find out how their career in sport began and developed.'

How to plan and conduct an in-depth interview

1 Contact the person you would like to interview. Tell them why you wish to interview them and how long it is likely to take, and then ask their permission to do so.

2 Plan the interview out carefully before the day.

- where will it take place?
- what do you want to know?
- how will you start the interview?
- make out a list of questions but be prepared to be flexible if the respondent's answers lead to other more interesting questions.

3 Decide beforehand how you are going to record the answers. A cassette recorder would be ideal, but check if the respondent is happy being recorded. Alternatively, take brief notes but try not to write continuously as this may put people off.

4 Conduct the interview with care. Start with straightforward, easy questions which will set a friendly atmosphere.

Speak clearly and vary the tone of your voice. Listen to the answers and respond to them in appropriate ways, e.g. nodding in agreement.

Let the interviewee finish his or her answer to a particular question before you begin to ask your next question.

Don't forget to thank the interviewee when the interview is at an end.

5   As soon as possible write up the interview. An appropriate way is to break up the interview into different headings and use the quotes from the ex-sportsman/woman as appropriate. If you do use quotes make sure that you get them exactly right as people are most unhappy if you misquote them.

Observation and experimentation

'When boys and girls take part in mixed sporting activities, are boys more competitive than when playing separately?'

This assignment could be tackled in a number of ways:

1   One way would be to observe directly a group of boys playing a game and compare their activities and responses when the same group plays the same game with a group of girls as well.

2   The same method could be employed except that this time you become part of the group and observe as you play. This is called **participant observation** and allows you to understand fully the group you are observing. Your conclusions should therefore be nearer to reality.

3   It may not be possible for you to see a group of boys playing first by themselves and then with a group of girls in the same sporting activity. It might be necessary to set up an experimental situation.

You will need the permission and assistance of your teacher/tutor in order for this experiment to be conducted.

4   Try not to influence the behaviour of the people that you are observing.

5   Analyse your results and write up your conclusions.

Whatever method is used to tackle this assignment, a number of points are common to them all.

● Discuss the approach with your teacher/tutor.
● Determine carefully what it is that you wish to observe.
● Ensure that it is safe and permissible to observe the groups of pupils.
● Decide how you are going to record your observations. You will find it quite difficult to observe and record at the same time. A method of shorthand, note-taking or ticksheet is most useful. The use of video camera would allow fuller analysis at a later stage.

Secondary data

'Discuss how sport and leisure activities are taking a more and more important role in the life of people in this country.'

In order to answer this question properly, it would first be necessary to establish that sport and leisure activities *are* taking a more important role in people's lives than in the past.

You would need evidence of participation levels, national and local government spending on sport and leisure, growth in sports facilities etc. This would entail gathering existing information, or secondary data.

Secondary data can be obtained from a whole variety of sources including official statistics, newspapers, books, television and radio programmes, videos, letters, diaries and a range of historical documents. Official statistics are produced by local and national government bodies. Information about sport and leisure is contained in many of them.

If you want more help, then it is worth going to your local library for assistance. The librarian will have access to a great deal of local data on sports provisions and use as well as on national trends.

Make sure that you understand any statistics which you may use. Use them sparingly and be sure to acknowledge where you obtained them. Don't forget that they can often be misleading, so think about the implications carefully.

The media (television, radio, newspapers, magazines etc.) are an excellent source of up-to-date information and views on sport.

It is worthwhile starting a collection of interesting articles, photos and recordings on sport and leisure. You never know when you may be able to make use of them in your assignments.

Do not accept all you may read or hear at face value. As the earlier chapter 'Sport reported' demonstrated, some of the information given in newspapers may be biased or distorted.

Books on sport abound. They range from autobiographies of famous sportsmen and sportswomen, through books on refereeing and coaching to specialist texts on the psychology of winning in team sports. They can all be valuable sources of information and opinion.

Historical novels can give you an insight into sporting activities in the past (e.g. Tom Brown's Schooldays) whilst copies of *Which?* can give you an up-to-date insight into spending patterns on sports equipment.

Finally, don't forget to contact the specialist sporting organisations which exist to promote sport and leisure activities. These are listed in appendix 3.

How to present information

A number of the sports assignments require you to gather information from a wide variety of sources. At a later stage you may need to display this information in order to present a case or support a cause.

It is important that your presentation is clear and easy to understand.

For example, imagine you have obtained the following information which gives the results of a survey given to 120 15-year-old girls asking which of the following sports they preferred to watch on television.

Athletics	30
Gymnastics	38
Cricket	8
Football	12
Hockey	20
Other sports	12

A **pie chart** could be used to display this information. A pie chart is a circular chart which is divided into slices or sectors of different sizes – the sizes being related to the proportion that each sector occupies of the total of all the sectors.

There is a total of 120 girls who made a choice of the sports offered to them.

As there are 360 degrees at the centre of a circle, then each girl is allocated $360 \div 120 = 3$ degrees.

The number of degrees allocated to each sport is shown in the chart below and then by means of a pie chart.

Sport	Number	Total number of degrees
Athletics	30	$3 \times 30 = 90$
Gymnastics	38	$3 \times 38 = 114$
Cricket	8	$3 \times 8 = 24$
Football	12	$3 \times 12 = 36$
Hockey	20	$3 \times 20 = 60$
Other sports	12	$3 \times 12 = 36$
Total girls	120	
Total degrees		360

TV Survey on 120 15-year-old girls

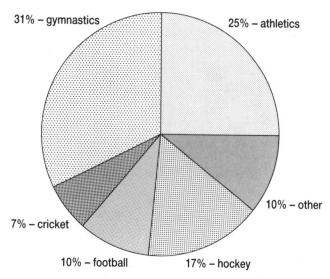

It is also possible to explode either one or all sections of the pie chart in order to create a better effect. This will require much more accuracy on your part. Of course if you are able to use one of the many computer graphics software packages now available the task becomes very much easier.

TV Survey on 120 15-year-old girls

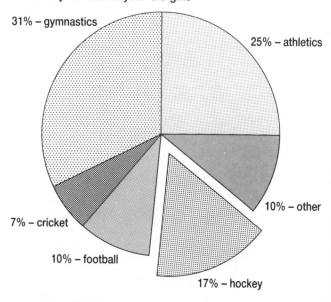

A fully exploded pie chart:

TV Survey on 120 15-year-old girls

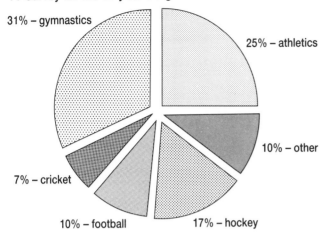

The results of the survey could also be shown by means of a **bar chart**:

TV Survey on 120 15-year-old girls

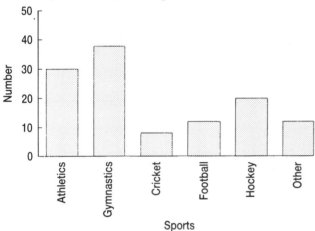

The bar chart can also be drawn horizontally as shown below:

TV Survey on 120 15-year-old girls

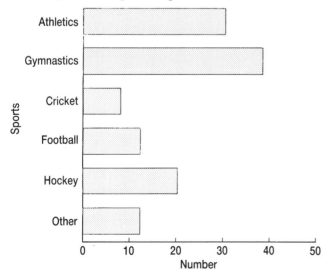

Yet another way of presenting information is by means of a **pictogram**. Decide upon a symbol to represent a defined quantity of the information to be displayed. Then display the appropriate number of the chosen symbol to represent the totals for each category. For example the following pictogram could be used to display our TV survey data.

TV Survey on 120 15-year-old girls

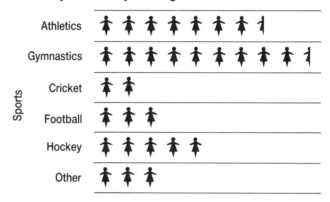

Key 🚶 = 4 girls

If the data which you have gathered are continuous (for example the height or weight of a group of people) then it is also possible to display the data by means of a **line graph**. In a line graph it is assumed that it is possible to have a score at any point along the line. It is easy to see that it is reasonable to expect people to weigh 70 kilos, 71 kilos or any point between these two weights. In the case of our TV survey it does not make any sense to say that 21 girls said that their favourite television was half-way between cricket and football. A line graph would therefore be meaningless in this case.

The line graph below shows an athlete's heart rate taken every 30 seconds for 240 seconds starting immediately at the end of a session of interval training.

Athlete's heart rate immediately after interval training

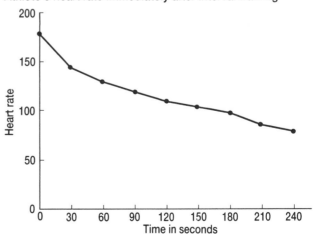

Practise using these methods by carrying out the following assignment:

Display the following information by means of:

(a) a pie chart
(b) a bar chart
(c) a pictogram

Take care in the choice of scales for each of these tasks.

A physiotherapist dealt with the following injuries over the period of three months.

Back   30
Knee   25
Ankle   20
Shoulder muscles   16
Upper leg muscles   9

Useful addresses

BODYTALK
The National Fitness Trade Journal
Bodytalk Communications House
168 Church Road
Hove
Sussex BN3 2DL
(publish bi-monthly magazine)

British Olympic Association
1 Wandsworth Plain
London SW8 1EH

Central Council for Physical Recreation
Francis House
Francis Street
London SW1P 1DE

The Institute of Baths and Recreation Management
    Incorporated
Giffard House, 36–38 Sherrard Street
Melton Mowbray
Leics LE13 1XJ
(publish bi-monthly magazine)

The Institute of Leisure and Amenity Management
Victoria House
25 High Street
Over
Cambridge CB4 5NB
(publish monthly magazine)

National Coaching Foundation
4 College Close
Beckett Park
Leeds LS6 3QH

The Physical Education Association of GB and NI
Ling House
162 Kings Cross Road
London WC1X 9DH

The Centre Manager
Picketts Lock Centre
Picketts Lock Lane
Edmonton
London N9 0AS

Safesport
Hawkflex Ltd
47 Holland Park Mews
London W11 3SP
(publish magazine 6 times per year)

Scenefit
Headway Publications Ltd
Clareville House
47 Whitcomb Street
London WC2H 7DX
(publish bi-monthly magazine)

Serve and Volley
The Lawn Tennis Association
Queens Club
West Kensington
London W14 9EG
(publish magazine 4 times per year)

The Sports Council
16 Upper Woburn Place
London WC1H 0QP

Sports Documentation Scheme
Main Library
University of Birmingham
Birmingham B15 2TT

Sports Industry
PO Box 13
Hereford House
Bridle Path
Croydon CR9 4NL
(publish monthly magazine)

Sportsworld International
3 Bloemfontein Avenue
London W12 7BH
(publish monthly magazine)

Stoners Buildings Limited
Priestley Way
Crawley
Sussex RH10 2PR

Work-Out
The Body and Health Magazine
72–80 Leather Lane
London EC1N 7TR
(publish monthly magazine)

Sports Council National Centres

Bisham Abbey National Sports Centre
Nr Marlow
Buckinghamshire SL7 1RT
Tel: 062 84 76911
Director: Bev Stephens

Crystal Palace National Sports Centre
Norwood
London SE19 2BB
Tel: 01 778 0131
Director: John Davies

Holme Pierrepont National Water Sports Centre
Adbolton Lane
Home Pierrepont
Nottingham NG12 2LU
Tel: 0602 821212
Director: Dennis Rodgers

Lilleshall Hall National Sports Centre
Nr Newport
Shropshire TF10 9AT
Tel: 0952 603003
Director: Derek Tremayne

Plas y Brenin National Centre for Mountain Activities
Capel Curig
Gwynedd
North Wales
Tel: 069 04 214 (Office)
Director: Dave Alcock

Northern Region
Aykley Heads
Durham DH1 5UU
Tel: 091 384 9595
Director: Bill Saunders

North West Region
Astley House
Quay Street
Manchester M3 4AE
Tel: 061 834 0338
Acting Director: Brian Parry

Yorkshire and Humberside Region
Coronet House
Queen Street
Leeds LS1 4PW
Tel: 0532 436443/4
Director: Cyril Villiers

East Midland Region
Grove House
Bridgford Road
West Bridgford
Nottingham NG2 6AP
Tel: 0602 821887 and 822586
Director: Terry Mack

West Midlands Region
Metropolitan House
1 Hagley Road
Five Ways
Birmingham B16 8TT
Tel: 021 454 3808/9
Director: David Pryor

Eastern Region
26 Bromham Road
Bedford MK40 2QP
Tel: 0234 45222
Director: Chris Clark

Greater London and South East Region
PO Box 480
Crystal Palace National Sports Centre
Ledrington Road
London SE19 2BQ
Tel: 01 778 8600
Director: John Birch

Southern Region
51A Church Street
Caversham
Reading
Berkshire
Tel: 0734 483311
Director: Laurie Bridgeman

South Western Region
Ashlands House
Ashlands
Crewkerne
Somerset TA18 7LQ
Tel: 0460 73491
Director: Peter Barson

There are also autonomous national sports councils in the three other UK countries, at these addresses:

SCOTLAND
The Scottish Sports Council
1 St Colme Street
Edinburgh EH3 6AA
Tel: 031 225 8411

WALES
The Sports Council for Wales
The National Sports Centre for Wales
Sophia Gardens
Cardiff CF1 9SW
Tel: 0222 397571

NORTHERN IRELAND
The Sports Council for Northern Ireland
House of Sport
Upper Malone Road
Belfast BT9 5LA
Tel: 0232 661222